JUST DREAMING

Just Dreaming

Joe Amico

iUniverse, Inc.
Bloomington

Just Dreaming

iUniverse books may be ordered through booksellers or by contacting:

iUniverse
1663 Liberty Drive
Bloomington, IN 47403
www.iuniverse.com
1-800-Authors (1-800-288-4677)

ISBN: 978-1-4759-6512-4 (sc)
ISBN: 978-1-4759-6511-7 (hc)
ISBN: 978-1-4759-6510-0 (e)

Library of Congress Control Number: 2012922769

Printed in the United States of America

iUniverse rev. date: 12/27/2012

Contents

Introduction

I FEEL COMPELLED TO give the reasons why I needed to write this book. I have been interested in history and politics since I can remember. I was born in Chicago on November 4, 1949. My parents were first-generation Sicilians. My mother didn't finish high school because she had to work in her parents' small grocery store on the corner of Hobbie Street and Cleveland Street in Chicago. My father managed to get through high school and even took some college courses. His father had abandoned him, his two sisters, and his two brothers when he was in his early teenage years.

Being a baby boomer, my first recollection of politics was the 1960 presidential campaign. I knew little about world events, but my father was a political junkie and often talked politics at home. He was a staunch conservative and was a Nixon supporter. However, we were Catholics, and John F. Kennedy was being vilified for his religion. This created a dilemma for my father. He hated liberals but knew that the criticism of Kennedy's religion was unfair. I assume he voted for Nixon but I could see that he was conflicted.

I remember being in ninth grade at Pius X High School in Paramount, California, when an announcement came over the intercom that President Kennedy had been assassinated. This had a profound effect on me. I didn't know that much about politics but admired JFK. I was moved by the things he said and believed that he was a great man. His death and the following controversy surrounding his assassination drew me to politics. I was convinced that Oswald did not act alone and even debated a teacher about the facts of the case. This event turned me into a skeptic regarding politics and government.

By the time the 1964 election came around, I was fully engaged in history and politics. I was a Barry Goldwater supporter. I was drawn to his populist philosophy and was convinced that Lyndon B. Johnson had something to do with the Kennedy assassination. I actively campaigned for Goldwater, making phone calls and passing out pamphlets. The Vietnam War was just starting to escalate, but at the time I really did not understand all of the war's implications or the effect it would have on me. I remember watching the convention on television with my father and being very impressed with a speech given by Ronald Reagan. I also remember that Goldwater was being painted as a "warmonger" who would escalate the war in Vietnam.

Of course, Johnson won in a landslide and escalated the war. As I drew closer to draft age, the war was all my friends and I could talk about. I was certain about one thing: I did not want to become a soldier. I could not understand why the government would want to send us thousands of miles from home to kill people living in grass huts and working in rice paddies. The more I read about this war, the more I grew to detest the needless slaughter that was taking place.

I graduated high school in 1967 and enrolled in Compton Junior College in Compton, California. My high school had been primarily Caucasian and Hispanic. There were virtually no African Americans. Compton College was my first experience with black culture. I was very aware of the civil rights movement and was a big fan of Martin Luther King Jr., but I did not have any face-to-face experiences with blacks. For the most part, I found little difference in the day-to-day interactions of my fellow students, but there was an underlying tension that I could not quite put my finger on.

I became good friends with Mr. Brown, a black professor who was born in Africa and spoke with a very proper English accent. Mr. Brown took me under his wing and spent a generous amount of his time going over current events. This was a time of much social turmoil. The Black Student Union had a strong following at Compton, and Mr. Brown was a sponsor of that organization. He would often invite me to meetings despite the protest of the members. Mr. Brown insisted that I be able to attend the meetings and threatened to withdraw his sponsorship if I was barred. Since all organizations on campus needed a faculty advisor and Mr. Brown was the only teacher willing to sponsor them, I was finally allowed to attend.

These meetings strongly influenced my thinking and understanding of race issues. I was given an opportunity that very few people of my background could experience. It was an education far beyond the parameters of regular classes. I was very appreciative of Mr. Brown's incredible knowledge and guidance and the insights that were given to me.

The country was in turmoil. The war in Vietnam was escalating by the day, the civil rights movement and feminism were in full swing, young people were "tuning out and turning on," and all the paradigms this country was built on were coming into question. There was a social revolution unlike anything the country had seen before.

Then on April 4, 1968, Martin Luther King Jr. was assassinated. This was a huge blow to the gut. It was hard to put into words. Attending a primarily black college at that time in history was like being in the epicenter of a storm. I never personally felt threatened but could see in the face of my fellow students anger, sadness, depression, and all the other feelings that must have been experienced that fateful day. We spent many hours processing this event and what it meant in the greater scheme of things.

This assassination added more fuel to the firestorm of discontent with the American way of life and all the values this country was built on. The war was now raging, and some of my friends who were drafted or enlisted were either killed or came back so damaged emotionally that they could barely function. I became actively involved in antiwar activities and the civil rights movement, and I considered myself a staunch feminist. I was immersed in the politics of the day and could see only one answer: social revolution.

Lyndon Johnson decided not to run again for president, which was an obvious choice. He had lied to the American people and was responsible for the deaths of thousands of people. The country was on the verge of social upheaval and desperately needed new leadership. One of the few candidates whom I felt myself drawn to was Bobby Kennedy. He represented himself in a way that I could identify with, promised to end the war, had a strong civil rights background, and seemed to understand the plight of the lower echelon of society.

Once again a significant leader was assassinated. This was almost too much for me to take. What kind of country did I live in? How could this happen? I was inconsolable. Mr. Brown tried to put things in perspective for me. He tried to convince me that the system was so threatened by the change that was happening that they had become desperate. I couldn't give up. I knew that what he was telling me was right, but I was hurting (and still hurt to this day).

As I remember it, my generation was questioning the system that allowed for war, racism, sexism, and the materialism most of us bathed ourselves in. We questioned our parents' generation in a way that had no parallel in history. I was convinced that my generation would make significant changes in the very nature of the system. Boy, was I wrong! Once the Vietnam War ended and we brought the last troops home in April 1975, most of those who were involved in protesting were in their late twenties or early thirties and had to get busy with life. They needed to get jobs and raise a family.

Unfortunately, the economy was in disarray. Inflation reached 13.3 percent by 1979, and interest rates were at an all-time high. There was no more time for philosophizing; we had to go to work. Not only did we abandon our ideals, we made our parents' generation look like loafers. We were willing to work sixty or seventy hours a week in order to afford the material goods that cost our parents a third of what it cost us.

As I see it, we have come to a crossroads in history. We can continue on the path we are currently on, which is war, mass consumption of the world's limited resources, jingoism, and fighting over the crumbs offered to us, or we can rekindle the vision we had and set out on a new path.

This book is my way of saying there is a much better way of doing things, and it has already been laid out for us. All we need to do is revisit the principles that our country was founded on and let what we know to be the truth become reality.

CHAPTER ONE

Dreams

IT WAS AN UNCOMFORTABLY warm, stuffy day. The usual trade winds were not offering me any relief as I sat in my apartment. Fortunately, I live a short distance from the beach, so I decided to grab a towel and a book, and I began my search for some cooler air.

Once I arrived at my destination, I realized I had made the right decision. It was one of those perfect Maui days. There was a gentle breeze from the north. The island of Lanai was straight ahead, the West Maui Mountains to my right, Haleakala behind me, and a white sandy beach to either side. No matter how many times I came to this spot, I found it more beautiful with each visit.

I went to my favorite spot, placed my beach towel down on the soft sand, and eased into a comfortable position. I closed my eyes and felt the ocean breeze caressing my face as the waves steadily rolled onto shore. Before I knew it, I had dozed off. I must have been dreaming, because when a beach ball hit me squarely on the nose, it took me a few seconds to realize where I was.

I had been napping for only a few minutes, but in that short time I was transported to the world of dreams. I could not remember anything about my dream, but I knew my mind had taken me somewhere else. I marveled at all the places dreams had taken me. What a wonderful thing dreams are—not that I always dreamt about wonderful things, but there is something so magical about them.

I was not concerned about the scientific nature of dreams, only the wondrous ways they transported me to mysterious places. Dreams? What are they? Where do they come from? Are they images that have been stored in our brain, reconfigured, and brought back to us while we are sleeping?

I was wondering if human beings had always had dreams. What did prehistoric people dream about? The more complex life has gotten, the more complex dreams must have gotten. As humans evolved, their dreams also must have evolved. Dreams must have played a significant role in the development of our species.

As I lay there thinking about dreams and where they came from, an elderly man came up to me and asked me what time it was. I looked at my watch and realized that I had been on the beach for over an hour. I asked myself where the time had gone; I had spent the last hour either dreaming in my sleep or daydreaming about dreams.

There are several meanings to the word "dream." The first definition is a series of thoughts, images, or emotions occurring during sleep. The second definition is an experience of waking life having the characteristics of a dream. The third definition is a visionary creation of the imagination. Dreaming while asleep, dreaming while awake, and daydreaming all happen unconsciously. In other words, daydreaming is the process by which one's mind wanders off on its own.

The fourth type of dreaming is conscious dreaming. Conscious dreaming is our ability to let our imagination see things that are not there. We choose our dreams, which are driven by our imagination. This type of dreaming is a very powerful tool for changing our reality. As a matter of fact, without the ability to dream, we could not improve our lot in life. Dreams are our aspirations, ambitions, and desires.

All that we have was created in someone's dreams. Dreams are a prerequisite to improvement. Without dreams, we would be stuck in the present, never being able to look toward a future. Dreaming unlocks the door to our imagination, which can create an infinite number of possibilities.

Before there was an airplane, someone had to dream that such a thing was possible. For centuries, people dreamt about being able to fly. Many brilliant minds set about building a craft that would allow them to fly. For centuries, these contraptions failed, but because the dream continued to live in people's minds, one day someone actually succeeded and turned their dream into reality. They saw in their mind's eye a machine that would defy the laws of gravity and lift them into flight. Science, art, music, and all that we have accomplished as human beings is the result of someone's dreams.

Our dreams, to a large extent, determine who we are. Dreams determine how we live. We are limited only by our ability to dream. If we can dream it, then we can do it. Dreams are a very powerful force in our lives, and the major advantage is that our dreams are our own personal property. Nobody can take away our right to dream. Every human being on earth has the right to dream.

While dreams are limited only by our imagination and can be anything we want them to be, acting on our dreams is another matter. Dreams, although a useful escape at times, have little meaning if we cannot act on them and create them into reality.

If dreaming is the ability to see things that are not there, then creating is the ability to take those dreams and turn them into reality.

We are creative beings. We have the need to create. Dreaming is the fuel that drives us to be creative. Dreams and creativity are two equal partners. Dreams without the ability to create would be useless, and the ability to create without dreams would not be possible.

Dreams and the ability to create are equal partners but have very different natures. Dreaming has no limits. Anyone can dream of anything their imagination will allow. The ability to create has some basic limitations. One of those limitations is our ability. Many people dreamt of building a machine that could fly, but not all were successful. Whether it was their lack of knowledge of basic physics, lack of resources, or just plain laziness, it took the right set of circumstances before there was success. Just because a person dreams of something does not guarantee success.

One limitation in creating our dreams into reality is the rules and limits placed on us by the society in which we live. Not every dream can be realized. If I dreamt of one day becoming king of the United States of America, my dream could never be realized. Some societies are more conducive to creativity than others. The fewer restrictions placed on us by society, the more likely we could create our dreams into reality.

Another consideration in creating a dream into reality is our ability to convince others of the value or purpose of our dream. In order for us to create our dreams into reality, we need the cooperation of others. We must share our dream or vision with others before we can be successful. Alexander Graham Bell dreamt of a communication system where voices could be transmitted across a wire. For that to happen, he had to first prove that such a thing was possible, and then he needed the cooperation of others, both financially and physically, to change the way we communicated with each other. While the dream was clearly his, he needed other people to understand his dream and help him create it into a reality.

All inventions, both great and small, are a result of someone's dream. The world we live in is the result of people's dreams. However, without the cooperation of many individuals or a shared dream, things can never really change. Our way of life, government, laws, economy, transportation system, and health-care system all were initiated in someone's dreams.

Our Founding Fathers had to have imagined the kind of society they wanted to create. They shared that vision with others until they had a consensus, and then they set out to create their vision into reality. It took many thousands of people to join forces and overcome overwhelming odds to create their shared dream.

Shared dreams and individual dreams are dependent on each other. They must work in partnership. If people stopped dreaming of a better world for themselves and others, conditions would never improve. If conditions never improved, then people would be limited in their ability to dream and thus their ability to create. If my dream was to live in a world free from disease and the world around me was filled with disease, my dream would not be possible. I would need to share my dream with others and work together to create a disease-free environment. We are interdependent beings, and dreams are the glue that holds us together.

Dreaming is the most powerful tool we humans have to improve our conditions. Once we stop dreaming, we stop improving. Without dreams, we have no goals. We would be merely existing with no purpose in life. To stop dreaming would be a form of suicide. It would be a death of sorts, because nothing would ever change.

Where there are no dreams, there is only sadness and misery. Dreams are nature's gift to help us rejoice in our humanness.

To limit dreams is to limit our ability to be human and share in all the wonders of the universe. Dreams are our right as human beings.

Laws can be enacted to restrict our ability to create. Laws can never be enacted to restrict our ability to dream. Dreams can only be restricted by our own imaginations. It is true that social conditions can be so oppressive that we forget that we can dream. We can become so involved in our daily lives that all we can see is our everyday existence. When we complain about the world as it is—the crime, the cost of living, big government, high taxes—we need to remember that our only way of remedying our situation is to dream of the kind of world we want to live in and then work together to create that world. The world could be anything we want it to be as long as we have the ability to dream!

CHAPTER TWO

The American Dream

"But there has been also the American Dream, that dream of a land in which life be should better and richer and fuller for every man, with opportunity for each according to his ability or achievement. It is a difficult dream for European upper class to interpret adequately, and too many of ourselves have grown weary and mistrustful of it. It is not a dream of motor cars and high wages merely, but a dream of social order in which each man and woman shall be able to attain to the fullest stature of which they are innately capable, and be recognized by others for what they are regardless of fortuitous circumstances of birth or position."

James Truslow Adams

DREAMS ARE DREAMS ARE dreams. The mother of all dreams is the American dream. The American dream changed the world like no other dream. The American dream changed the course of history. It is the best example of a collective dream, a dream so powerful that it is known by millions of people from every corner of the globe, a dream that has drawn millions of people to it like moths to a light. It is a dream so seductive that one of this country's major social problems is trying keeping people from penetrating its boundaries to share in its wonder.

For those of us who have been lucky enough to be born in the United States, we are indeed fortunate. We have our very own dream. It is unique to the world. No one ever refers to "the European dream" or "the Asian dream." People from those places certainly have dreams. It's just that before the New World was happened upon by Western civilization, people were very restricted regarding what type of life they could dream of and create for themselves. People were essentially born into their station in life. There was a system of hierarchy and despotic rule. In these social systems, everyone knew their place and agreed to live within the established order of things. The average person's dreams could never be realized. If your parents were poor and you had dreams of becoming rich, you had little or no chance of realizing your dreams. If anything, dreams were very dangerous to the common person. If the common person dreamt of joining the hierarchy and attempted to do so, they would most likely lose their head.

Before the American dream, people's lives were very restricted. The hierarchy owned and controlled the land and resources. Taxes were collected to serve the rich. The ruling class controlled every aspect of a person's life. What type of home a person lived in, how they would make their living, what type of education, if any, were all determined by the ruling class. Even a person's relationship with their God was determined by the ruling class.

The ruling class had absolute power and enforced that power with absolute authority. To defy the ruling class meant certain imprisonment or death. The ruling class had complete economic control because they owned all the land and natural resources. People were merely allowed to live on their property and had to pay dearly for the privilege to do so. They could only accumulate as much wealth as the ruling class would permit.

At this point in history, dreams were a source of pain for the common person because they could not realize them. They could never realize their dreams because they had no political rights. People were not free to vote; they could not assemble with their neighbors to discuss their conditions. To do these things in defiance of the accepted social order would have serious consequences. The ruling class had large standing armies and powerful navies to enforce their absolute power over the common person.

Along with economic and political control, the ruling class also controlled a person's religious beliefs. The church and state were essentially the same thing. The king was often the leader of the church or was in direct control of the head of the church. People could not be trusted to find their own spiritual being, because those beliefs might undermine the accepted social order. Religion was the tool of the ruling class to control the masses. If people were allowed to find their God in their own way, they would be free to dream and create a new reality. Those who worshipped a God not sanctioned by the anointed ruler were persecuted for those beliefs. Prior to the "discovery" of the "New World," dreams were somewhat pointless.

It is true that a "renaissance" was taking place around the time the Americas were "discovered." People of great vision began to flourish. Art, music, and philosophy began to grow, but the idea of individual freedoms was just being introduced. The Magna Carta was forced upon the king of England, and while it only applied to a percentage of the population, the rumbling of freedoms for the common person were in the making.

Many events took place during this period in time that introduced the power of dreams to a stagnant world. Among these events was the invention of the printing press. This made reading materials available to a larger segment of the population. More and more people learned to read and write. Print made the "word" more powerful than the "sword." Dreams of a better way of doing things were written about. People began to dream of a better world.

Columbus had a dream that he could find a shorter route to the rich Eastern countries. He shared this dream with the queen of Spain, convinced her of his vision, and set sail to realize his dream. Little did he know that when he first saw the San Salvador Islands in 1492, his journey would change the course of human history.

The discovery of the New World changed dramatically the way people viewed their existence. The invention of the printing press and the discovery of the New World were the fuses that lit the fire of the American dream. It is difficult to put into context the impact on the human psychological makeup these two events had. It was as if the power of dreams were trapped in a bottle. Columbus's adventure uncorked that bottle and let the genie out. The largest migration of human beings in human history began to take place. For the first time, people could dream of a better life for themselves and their families; with hard work, courage, and a lot of luck, they could turn their dreams into reality.

It was as if Columbus had discovered another planet. Imagine if one of our space journeys resulted in the discovery of a planet that was totally undeveloped, a place where a person could carve out a piece of land for themselves and create a life for themselves and their families, a land so rich in natural resources that the only thing that limited a person was their ability to dream and act on those dreams. That was the dream that was let out of the bottle in 1492.

The tidal wave of dreams that was unleashed completely overwhelmed the natives of this "new" land. People were driven by the dream of being free to create their own life, to worship their own God, and to have all the good things that life had to offer. The fact that the land that they had "discovered" was occupied was a mere detail. The need to live free made it easy to justify the destruction of the native people and their cultures. For the first time, people were free to dream, and they would do anything to secure that freedom. The natives were no match for the technology of death the white man used with such great lust.

The way the natives saw the world was very different than the way the white man saw the world. The natives held beliefs that put them in harmony with nature. They believed that nature could not be controlled or altered. Nature provided the native peoples with all that they needed, so they found little need to change their environment. The white man believed that nature could and should be controlled. The two views were in direct conflict with each other. It was inevitable that the desire to control nature would dominate the desire to live in harmony with nature.

Inherent in the desire to control is the use of violence. In order for someone to force their views or beliefs on another person, they must use violence (or the threat of violence). Violence was the primary method used to conquer the New World. The greater the need to control, the greater the need for violence.

It is not my purpose to judge the right and wrong of the way the Europeans treated the indigenous people of the New World. It is only to point out that once people were free to dream and act on those dreams, nothing could stand in their way.

As more people from Europe came to the New World to realize their dreams, the more they came into conflict with the native people. Perhaps no greater dream existed for these immigrants than to own their own land. To own your own land meant you could control your own destiny. In the New World, there were millions of square miles of rich, undeveloped land, free for the taking. As more people came to the New World, more land was taken from the native people.

In the early stages of the American dream, people were self-sufficient. Ironically, with the help of the native people, they learned to extract enough from nature to survive. They hunted, fished, and grew their own food. Most importantly, they had dreams. They could worship their God in any fashion they wished. They were in control of their own destiny.

The American dream had little need for government. People had a basic mistrust of government, and who could blame them? They had come from a place where governments had trampled their dreams. People had little or no say as to how they were governed, and they had no desire to trust any government.

Once the dream had a foothold, nothing could stop it. Still more people came to live their dreams. People became farmers, tradespeople, ranchers, importers, and exporters. Because of the self-reliant nature of the dream, government remained small and played a minor role in the American dream. People learned to rely on each other to secure the things that made life worth living. What people could not create for themselves, they traded with their neighbors for.

More and more people came to share in the dream. There were basically two types of people who came to the New World. There were those who were following their dreams to create a new life for themselves, and those who were forced to come to be used as a cheap labor source. Slaves were brought by those who wanted to recreate the hierarchical system from which they came.

The ruling classes of the Old World naturally wanted to extend their rule to the New World. However, even though they had great armies and navies, they were no match for the American dream. People refused to go back to the old way of doing things. They didn't need or want a government, thousands of miles away, to tell them what to do. The dream to be free was the most powerful force unleashed in human existence, and nothing was going to stand in its way. After the American Revolution, the American dream became official government policy.

Still more people came, and new territories were carved out of the wilderness. Cities began to spring up. These cities became centers of trade and commerce. People who could never before have any chance of realizing their dreams were now self-reliant and living their dreams.

As more people were drawn to the New World by the dream, less land became available. America is a very large country, but by the end of the 1800s, much of the land had become private property. The New World was in transition from an agrarian society to an industrial society.

What ended the agrarian culture and shifted it to an industrial culture was the development of the assembly line. For the first time, material goods could be mass-produced in large quantities. This made goods affordable for the average person.

As land became less and less available and the means of production became more and more centralized, the American dream went through a transformation. Instead of the self-reliant farmer who had little need of government, it became necessary for people to earn money. In order to make money, people had to leave their farms and work in factories to earn a wage so they could afford to buy many of the things they formerly produced themselves.

The dream became dependent on a person's ability to make money. The only way to participate in the American dream was to make money. The more money an individual was able to earn, the more of the dream they could realize.

Another by-product of the industrialization of the dream was the dependency on fossil fuel. Fossil fuel is the lifeblood of the industrial era. As cities grew and factories sprang up, millions of people migrated to the United States to get their piece of the dream. The more people who came to share in the dream, the need to produce more and more goods grew. The more goods that were produced, the greater the need for fossil fuel.

The dream became dependent on the acquisition of material goods and the consumption of fossil fuel. The New World was blessed with an abundant supply of fossil fuel, but it soon became apparent that other sources of fuel would become necessary.

It is also important to note that while the Unites States was becoming an industrial nation, other countries followed suit. This put us in competition with other countries for the need for fossil fuels. The world economies became dependent on fossil fuels.

Things went humming along in this transition period from an agrarian society to an industrial society, and people migrated to the dream in a steady flow. While there were ups and downs in the new economy, things were "roaring" through the 1920s. Then, as if someone had popped a balloon, things came crashing down.

If ever there was a time when the American dream's great light flickered, it was during the Great Depression. The "Great Depression" is an accurate way of describing what happened on that fateful day of October 29, 1929. Millions of Americans were thrown into abject poverty. The dream was on the ropes, and things looked pretty bleak.

When the dream was agrarian, economic downturns did not have a devastating effect, because people were self-reliant and produced the goods they needed for a decent life. Once the dream became dependent on money for its realization, any downturn in the economy had serious consequences.

Not only was the American dream in a depression, the rest of the industrial nations were suffering the same fate. The world economy was in a freefall. A dark cloud was hanging over the world economies, and a storm was brewing.

As the Great Depression continued, the dream became dimmer and dimmer for more and more people. The government tried to revive the collapsed economy but had little success. What the industrial world needed was a product that could utilize the latest technology and have an unlimited demand, a product that would essentially become obsolete once it was consumed, thus ensuring its ongoing need. World War II was what was necessary to end the Great Depression.

All the industrialized nations that were caught up in the Great Depression blamed each other for their dismal condition. Tensions grew. The arms race was born. Factories that were closed down during this time were now retooled to produce military hardware. Tensions continued to grow until the world finally exploded.

The American dream was put on hold. All of those millions of unemployed men all over the world began killing each other. In total, over 50 million men, women, and children would die in this war. Those who were not killing each other were building weapons for those who were. The dream was at stake. People forgot about their economic condition and concentrated on killing each other.

During this war, weapons of mass destruction were being perfected. Technology advanced to the point that one weapon was developed that scared the hell out of everybody. With the use of this weapon, the war ended. Things began to settle down. Governments were restored. Societies began to rebuild.

The millions of people who were killing each other returned from the battlefield to their homes and families. Those who had fought for the dream and lived expected to reap the benefits of their sacrifices. They expected to share in the American dream. To share in the dream, they had to find jobs.

After the war was over, the world was separated into the good guys and the bad guys. We entered the Cold War, ensuring the production of military weapons and a large standing army. The name given to this is the "military industrial complex," which has employed millions of people and giving them an access to the dream.

People were anxious to get their share of the dream, so they would do almost anything to make money. An industry that could employee hundreds of thousands of people was necessary to keep the industrialization of the dream alive.

The major industry to provide well-paying jobs was the automobile industry. The automobile industry, and all its supporting industries, became the major sponsor of the dream. The automobile was the perfect "vehicle" to get people back to work. It required thousands of people in the factories that built the cars. It needed thousands of people to build the roads the cars would ride on.

Other industries sprang up from the automobile industry. The steel industry that was in full production during the war could continue producing steel for autos. The glass industry, the rubber industry, literally hundreds of peripheral industries, sprang up around the production of the automobile. It was useful that most of our industrial competitors had their infrastructure destroyed during the war, which gave us a head start in the growth of the auto industry.

Another major sponsor of the American dream was the fossil fuel industry. Fossil fuel production employed millions of Americans. The development of plastic and other synthetic materials firmly implanted the fossil fuel industry as a major sponsor of the dream.

Another sponsor of the dream was the technology industry. With the invention of the computer, Internet, and many other gadgets, a lot of people became rich and lived the dream.

After World War II, millions of people were able to live the industrialized version of the dream by working for a decent wage. Of course, there were millions of people who lived in poverty in the industrialized version of the dream. People of color, women, and the elderly were often excluded, but as someone observed, "Every poor American hoped to become rich, and every rich American was afraid of becoming poor."

The industrialization of the dream worked fairly well for a while until it hit another snag. The Cold War was heating up, and once again the world prepared for war. However, the development of nuclear weapons, or mutual self-destruction, as it was called, made fighting a major war impractical, so fighting limited wars became the new way of using the military industrial complex.

In 1954, the United States entered the Vietnam civil war. This was less than ten years after World War II ended and less than five years after the Korean "conflict." All of a sudden millions of young men, who came from relatively affluent homes, were ordered to go thousands of miles from their homes and kill people who lived in grass huts. This violent conflict was very different than World War II. The men of that war were unemployed, depressed, and desperate. To add to that, they had one of the most despised figures in history to fight. Hitler was the ultimate bad guy. It was clear that he was out to destroy everybody's dreams with his war machine, and he had to be stopped.

Vietnam was a very different story. The baby boomers, as they became known, were fairly well off. The industrialization of the dream was working for most white Americans. Most white people had jobs and were able to live a decent life.

Many of the boomers were able to go to college, because the government made higher education affordable. The boomers were not so anxious to go off to war. It was never clear why we were there. It was hard to see why people who lived in tiny grass huts, working in rice paddies, could be a threat to the dream.

As more and more body bags came back from Vietnam, it became apparent that the government had made a tragic mistake. Many boomers resisted the draft and protested the war. They began to question the industrialized version of the dream and rebelled against it.

Another blow against the industrialized version of the dream was occurring along with the protest of the war. Other segments of the population began to challenge the dream. It became apparent that the industrialized version of the American dream was not accessible to significant segments of the population. People of color, women, and others were discriminated against and did not have equal opportunity to share in the dream.

This was a very dark time for the industrialized version of the dream. Cities were being burned down. Students were rioting in the streets. Soldiers were shooting protesters. Political figures were being killed. The dream was being seriously questioned in a way it had never been before.

Once the situation became desperate, the leaders cut their losses and ran. They also pumped millions of dollars into the war on poverty to try and restore order to the inner cities and appease those who were discriminated against.

After the troops returned, they were faced with the reality of having to earn a living to support their families. People had to find a decent wage in order to live the dream. They needed to buy homes, cars, and all the other necessities to live the industrialized version of the dream. Unfortunately, things did not go smoothly.

After the military conflict, prices of all the necessities rose dramatically. Rising prices is one of those economic conditions that can really put a dent in the dream. When prices go up and unemployment goes up, fewer and fewer people have access to the dream. Once again the dream was in serious trouble. People were shooting each other in gas lines, and interest rates were through the roof.

When things looked their darkest, and as if by magic (or a Hollywood script), Ronald Reagan rode into town to save the day (and the dream). He did this in a unique way. After the unpopular Vietnam conflict, people had lost their stomach for war. Armed military conflict is an important tool of the dream, because it employs lots of people. However, Reagan came up with a solution. He pretended we were at war. He began to pump billions of dollars into the military industrial complex and raise tension with the commies. He was even heard to joke about dropping the bomb on our enemies. Once it became clear that Reagan would spend any amount of money to develop weapons to destroy the Soviets, they cried uncle. Once again, the dream was saved.

Since that time, there have been two serious recessions and the near collapse of the economy, which has not been resolved as of this writing. Once again the American dream is in serious jeopardy. It is my belief that as long as the American dream is tied to industry, we will always be chasing our tails. Fortunately, there is a document called the Declaration of Independence that sets forth the principles and ideals that encompass the true meaning of the American dream, not the industrialized version of it. The Declaration of Independence started us on our journey, and I believe that only it can save us in these dark times.

CHAPTER THREE

Rethinking the Dream

THIS BOOK IS NOT a historical document, though I refer to known historical events. It is not a scientific document, though I refer to accepted scientific facts. It is a book based on my own political and ideological beliefs that I feel are relevant to what is occurring in the world today.

The American dream: What is it? Where did it come from, and who has a right to it? The first time I remember hearing about the American dream, I was a small child and my father said, "Joey, you are very lucky to live in a country where you can be anything you want to be." I found this confusing, because it always felt like someone was always telling me what to do. My parents, teachers, bosses, someone was always telling me what to do and when to do it. I sure didn't feel like I could be anything I wanted to be.

I know that the American dream is a concept that attracted my grandparents from Sicily to find a better life for themselves and their families. It was a concept that my father passionately believed in, even though I saw him struggle to pay the bills and raise a family. I knew that there had to be some truth to the dream, but I could not understand its basic contradictions, so I set out to look for the origins of the dream in order to better understand it.

I began my search by referring back to the period in which the dream was born, a time when the ideas were framed and shaped into the American dream. I found inspirational words that seemed to reach out and grab me by my very soul.

I believed that in order for me to truly understand the American dream, I would have to find it in a document of such historical significance that it could not be disputed. That document is the Declaration of Independence. The Declaration of Independence is the dream's manifesto. It is the heartbeat of the dream. It is the roots from which all that the American dream offers grows. I believed that by looking deeply into the Declaration of Independence, by dissecting it word by word, I could find the true meaning of the American dream, which is supposedly our birthright.

I am convinced that without the Declaration of Independence, the American dream would not exist. To me, the Declaration of Independence is the most important document ever written. Its words changed the course of human existence. Its words had such power that they unleashed a tidal wave of human energy for all those who wanted to follow their dreams.

It included words such as "freedom," "equality," and "pursuit of happiness"; these words were so magical that they fired up the imaginations of people all over the world. These words ignited our ability to dream of a better life for ourselves and our children. These words gave us a guarantee. The Declaration is the foundation of the American dream and sets forth the principles to build a society on.

For the first time in history, a government was instituted to ensure the rights of people to share in the dream. Without a clear understanding of the Declaration of Independence, one cannot fully appreciate the American dream. At a time when there seems to be much discussion of what our Founding Fathers meant, or what kind of society they envisioned, the answer is right in front of us.

The Declaration of Independence is an amazingly short document, considering its effect on human development. It is also very clear as to its meaning. Each word carries with it a meaning that defines the American dream for us. One does not have to be a historian or a linguist to interpret it. There is no high priest or wizard who holds the key to its meaning. It is up to each one of us to read the Declaration of Independence and come to some sort of consensus as to its meaning.

Those of us that live in the United States are fortunate because, in theory, we have a guarantee to be able to share in American dream. In a time when the lines between the rich and poor are growing ever larger and the country seems more divided than any time since the Civil War, where can we turn for some guidance? When prices for basic necessities are rising faster than our paychecks, when higher education becomes less and less accessible, and when people have to go into such debt to afford such an education, it becomes a double-edged sword. When our children are not safe, terrorists want to kill us, endless wars are being fought. When millions of us are out of work either because they can't find a job or they just stopped looking. We have fragmented into colors, classes, sexes, ages, religions, and political ideologies. Our prisons are overflowing. Our leaders seem more concerned about blaming each other for our problems than focused on fixing them; where can we turn?

This book is written in the belief that the American dream is in serious trouble. Without some clarity soon and some clear vision as to what needs to be done, I fear the American dream may be lost forever. It will be lost to the millions of people that are forced into poverty and for those who have means but are so worried about protecting their stuff from the have-nots that their lives become intolerable.

I believe that our only chance is for we as a people to understand where we came from. My purpose is to revisit the meaning of the American dream and bring it into the twenty-first century. The American dream is perhaps the only concept that can save us. It is our "mission statement," our guiding light. It is the very foundation that our society has been built on! It is truly what makes us great.

Why do I believe understanding the American dream is so important? By their very nature, dreams are unlimited. They can be anything a person imagines them to be. They can be anything! That means that we can live in any type of world we want. The only thing required of us is to dream the kind of world we want and then make it happen.

The question is, does everybody have the same understanding as to exactly what the American dream is? This is where things get complicated. Since the American dream has never been clearly defined, how is it that it has such allure? Many people have inferred what the American dream means to them. It is a very personal thing and means different things to different people. I do not pretend to know what the American dream actually means. However, I do believe that having a clear understanding of the definition of the American dream will make it a lot easier to find a direction we as a people should be headed in. The American dream derives its power from the fact that it is a vision shared by the majority of people.

Chapter Four

The Industrialization of the Dream

THE AMERICAN DREAM HAS gone through changes from the time the first settlers came to the Americas. The initial pioneers experienced the American dream through unlimited possibilities. This was achieved because people had access to free land and were able to produce the goods and services necessary to live a good life, with little or no government interference. After we became an industrial culture, the dream became more about accumulating material wealth. In order to accumulate material goods, it became necessary to increase profits and reduce costs.

This shift in the American dream quickly created large industries in oil, steel, shipping, and other sectors that make up today's economy. This transformation was not subtle. Great wealth was being accumulated by people, including those known as "Robber Barons." My purpose is not to question whether this is good or bad but to observe the effect this economic shift had on the American dream.

In the beginning stages of the American dream, people had to work together to tame the New World. To a large extent, the native people, nature, and the settlers' own ignorance worked against them. They had to work together to build a successful life. It is important to note that the government at this time played a very minor role in maintaining the American dream.

After the industrialization of the American dream and the desire to accumulate material goods became the goal, the role of government profoundly changed. Those who wanted to build great economic power needed a strong centralized government to help solidify their positions.

Those who wanted to accumulate as many material goods as they possibly could began building great economic empires. These individuals had a tremendous influence in shaping governmental policy. The government and industry became partners in shaping how the average American lived.

The means of production fell into fewer and fewer hands. The more the economy became centralized and relied on large corporations, the more corporations relied on government. The two worked together to limit competition and control markets. The larger the share of the market a corporation controlled, the more profitable it became. The more profitable it became, the more influence it had over government.

One of the ironies of the transformation of the American dream to one of accumulating material goods was that some people needed to be successful and some needed to be failures. That's what makes it work. The industrialization of the dream is hierarchical by its nature. Wealth is concentrated in the hands of a small percentage of people. As one moves down the proverbial ladder of success, less wealth is available.

The dream of accumulation relies upon people's desire to climb the ladder of success, because there are very strict rules on exactly how one can climb up. Since it is so difficult to climb the ladder of success, we must be in competition with each other, because each rung of the ladder becomes smaller and smaller.

Most societies are hierarchical. What makes the American dream so powerful is that there is a ladder at all. The fact that we can compete against each other keeps the dream alive. A lot of different factors go into how high we can climb—some of them fair, some of them not so fair. Another irony of this desire to accumulate material things is that those who are at the bottom of the ladder must develop a greater desire to own material things than those who already have accumulated wealth. This is because those who live in poverty must ignore their condition and want things to keep them in line—even if their dreams are kept alive by their belief that they will win the lottery or Publishers Clearing House will come knocking!

Another consequence of the American dream being transformed from one of self-reliance to accumulating material things is that not only must individuals be in competition with each other, so must nations. The dream to accumulate material things requires natural resources. The more people accumulate material things, the more resources are needed. America had tremendous natural resources, but it was not enough to satiate the dream of accumulation.

In order for a nation to ensure its access to resources, it is necessary to have a large standing army and navy. All great economic powers throughout history relied on their armies and navies to gather resources for their ability to accumulate things. A large government is necessary to build a large military to ensure the accumulation of things.

This is the state of the American dream today. The American dream has been stolen from us. I believe that people want the same things. We want to be self-reliant. We want our families and friends to be safe and happy. I believe that the desire to accumulate material goods is a perversion of the American dream. We have lost our way. Fortunately, we have a document that encompasses the very soul of the dream, and only by a close examination of this document can we find our way back to the American dream.

CHAPTER FIVE

The Declaration of Independence

(An Interpretation)

A DECLARATION BY THE Representatives of the United States of America, in General Congress assembled, July 4, 1776:

WHEN IN THE COURSE OF HUMAN EVENTS, IT BECOMES NECESSARY FOR ONE PEOPLE TO DISSOLVE THE POLITICAL BANDS WHICH HAVE CONNECTED THEM WITH ANOTHER, AND TO ASSUME AMONG THE POWERS OF THE EARTH, THE SEPARATE AND EQUAL STATION TO WHICH THE LAWS OF NATURE AND OF NATURE'S GOD ENTITLE THEM, A DECENT RESPECT TO THE OPINIONS OF MANKIND REQUIRES THAT THEY SHOULD DECLARE THE CAUSES WHICH IMPEL THEM TO THE SEPARATION.

WE HOLD THESE TRUTHS TO BE SELF-EVIDENT, THAT ALL MEN ARE CREATED EQUAL; THAT THEY ARE ENDOWED BY THEIR CREATOR WITH CERTAIN INALIENABLE RIGHTS; THAT AMONG THESE ARE LIFE, LIBERTY, AND

THE PURSUIT OF HAPPINESS. THAT TO SECURE THESE RIGHTS, GOVERNMENTS ARE INSTITUTED AMONG MEN, DERIVING THEIR JUST POWERS FROM THE CONSENT OF THE GOVERNED; THAT WHENEVER ANY FORM OF GOVERNMENT BECOMES DESTRUCTIVE OF THESE ENDS, IT IS THE RIGHT OF THE PEOPLE TO ALTER OR TO ABOLISH IT, AND TO INSTITUTE A NEW GOVERNMENT, LAYING ITS FOUNDATION ON SUCH PRINCIPLES, AND ORGANISZING ITS POWERS IN SUCH FORM AS TO THEM SHALL SEEM MOST LIKELY TO EFFECT THEIR SAFETY AND HAPPINESS. PRUDENCE, INDEED, WILL DICTATE THAT GOVERNMENTS LONG ESTABLISHED SHOULD NOT BE CHANGED FOR LIGHT AND TRANSIENT CAUSES; AND ACCORDINGLY ALL EXPERIENCE HATH SHOWN THAT MANKIND ARE MORE DISPOSED TO SUFFER, WHILE EVILS ARE SUFFERABLE, THAN TO RIGHT THEMSELVES BY ABOLISHING THE FORMS TO WHICH THEY ARE ACCUSTOMED. BUT WHEN A LONG TRAIN OF ABUSES AND USURPATIONS, PURSUING INVARIABLY THE SAME OBJECT, EVINCES A DESIGN TO REDUCE THEM UNDER ABSOLUTE DESPOTISM, IT IS THEIR RIGHT, IT IS THEIR DUTY, TO THROW OFF SUCH GOVERNMENT, AND TO PROVIDE NEW GUARDS FOR THEIR FUTURE SECURITY …

The Declaration of Independence continues on to list the specific grievances against the king of England. However, I believe that the American dream can be found in this portion of the document. The Declaration of Independence puts forth the principles by which a society was to be built. It is not possible to know with any certainty exactly what the authors had in mind when they wrote these words. Indeed, it is known that these words had many "exceptions" when they were written. It is my contention that written words take on a life of their own. Their interpretation is the responsibility of the reader. How these words are interpreted determines what meaning we assign to the American dream.

The Declaration of Independence changed the course of human history. Never before had a political document have such a powerful effect on the human condition. Each word carries with it such power, such meaning, such clarity that only through them can there be any understanding of the nature of the dream.

As a citizen of the United States and as a person who believes that the American dream has been diluted to the point where it holds little meaning, I believe that only by going back to our roots can we ensure that the American dream is not lost forever.

The journey begins in the first sentence of the Declaration of Independence: "When in the course of human events, it becomes necessary for one people to dissolve the political bands which have connected them with another."

"When in the course of human events ..." An event is a happening, especially an important happening. In the course of our lives, events happen that change our circumstances, which in turn change our views. When these events happen and circumstances change, we must evaluate our situation. After we evaluate our situation, we determine a course of action. This is true for individuals as well as for "one people."

When a significant event happens in a person's life, it can change the course or path that person is on. If someone loses a job, or falls into poor health, or wins the lottery, it would probably change that person's life in a profound way.

What holds true for the individual also holds true for "one people." It would be ridiculous to assume that everybody in the United States is of one mind. The question becomes, what was meant by "one people"? Cicero, the Roman statesman and philosopher, wrote in *De Republica* that a people is "not any collection of human beings brought together in any sort of way, but an assemblage of them in large numbers associated in an agreement with respect to justice and a partnership for the common good." Using that definition of "people," it would seem that just as when significant events occur to an individual that change the course he or she is on, the same thing can happen when significant events happen to "one people" that change the course we are collectively on.

"TO DISSOLVE THE POLITICAL BANDS WHCH HAVE CONNECTED THEM WITH ANOTHER …" When two people decide to marry, they enter into an agreement to share their lives together. They agree upon certain ground rules, goals, lifestyles, and then live as one. Sometimes a significant event can happen that impacts their relationship negatively, and as a result they may decide to end their marriage. This would change their lives dramatically.

The same principle holds true for "one people." Each individual enters into an agreement with each other as to a code of conduct. We agree to behave in a certain manner. Governments are formed and laws are enacted that "band" us together. "Bands" are the laws that define our legal relationship with each other. Every law defines the individual's relationship to the whole. Because the "bands" that connected us to each other were determined by the hierarchy of England prior to the Declaration of Independence, they did not represent the will of "one people." Therefore, it became necessary for "one people" to redefine their "bands" to each other and "dissolve" their bands with the English hierarchy.

"AND TO ASSUME AMONG THE POWERS OF THE EARTH …" The American dream comes into clearer focus. These words are simple yet complex. The author of the Declaration of Independence must have chosen each of his words very carefully, so it is imperative to assign meaning to each word.

"Assume" means to take up or claim, to seize, to take for granted or true. "To assume" leaves little doubt that what is to follow is a right. "Among" means one of or surrounded by. To "assume among" is to claim or seize any or all of a particular thing. In this case it is to "assume among the powers of the earth." The earth is the planet on which we live. What are those powers that we are to assume among?

One of the definitions of "power" is a means of supplying energy. If we define the earth as the area in which man thinks of himself as living and acting, we are talking about our entire environment, which is made up of four substances: water, land, fire, and air. These four elements are of equal value. They are equal in that they work in harmony with each other and hang in a delicate balance to create our environment. All of the elements create energy or power and are of equal value. Human existence is dependent on the "powers of the earth."

As previously noted, I am not a scientist. However, I have a basic understanding of our environment and how things work. Take the first substance that makes up the "powers of the earth": the air. Air is the mixture of invisible, colorless, tasteless gases that surround the earth. The air or atmosphere is necessary for obvious reasons. We need to breathe in order to live. We also need our atmosphere to protect us from harmful rays emitted from the sun. The atmosphere acts as a filter to allow just the necessary sun's rays to allow life to exist on earth. Without that filter, life could not exist.

The other "POWERS OF THE EARTH" are solids, liquids, and heat. These powers were abundant when the Declaration of Independence was written. I am certain that those who signed this document could not have conceived of a time when the powers of the earth would be depleted. It was a time when there was plenty for everybody, with no limits in sight. The American dream was partly founded on the concept of abundance.

The American dream can only be realized in relationship with the "POWERS OF THE EARTH." If the New World had been a desolate, uninhabitable wasteland, there would be no American dream. The fact that the New World was overflowing in its powers is what gave people hope for a new way of life they could have never before realized. Once people could "assume among the powers of the earth," anything became possible.

We are dependent on the powers of the earth for our existence as "one people." How we use the powers of the earth defined us as "one people." It could be said that the powers of the earth provide all that is needed for people to live a happy, fulfilled life.

How "one people" choose to use the powers of the earth determines what kind of world we live in. When these words were written, the earth's powers were owned and controlled by an elite few, who did what they willed with them. When the powers of the earth were owned and reserved for the few, life was hard and dreams were useless. Once the powers of the earth were to be shared by "one people," everyone could dream of a better world.

The American dream is dependent on how the powers of the earth are used. The more of the earth's powers one can access, the freer and more secure we become. What makes the words "to assume among the powers of the earth" so important is that for the first time in human existence, those powers of the earth belonged to everybody.

"THE SEPARATE AND EQUAL STATION TO WHICH THE LAWS OF NATURE AND OF NATURE'S GOD ENTITLE THEM ..."

Another big step in defining the American dream is taken with these words. The first interesting word is "separate." Its literal definition is to set apart or divide from the rest or others, is thought of or regarded as having individual form. In other words, individuality! To be recognized as an individual. Part of the American dream is the individual's right to control his or her own destiny.

"AND EQUAL STATION ..." The word "equal" appears twice in the Declaration of Independence. This first use of the word is in conjunction with the word "station." "Station" means a place or position to which something or someone stands or is assigned to stand and remain. Each person is assigned a station as "one people," and that station is equal to all others.

So we are separate entities but of equal stature. No other word has so divided or challenged the American dream than the word "equal."

"TO WHICH THE LAWS OF NATURE ..." At the time that the Declaration of independence was written, the average person was a farmer, tradesperson, merchant, or slave/indentured servant. People had to be in tune with the laws of nature, because their very survival depended on these laws. They could not yet manipulate nature with electricity or internal combustion engines.

They must have understood that the powers of the earth and the laws of nature were interdependent. Using the definition of the powers of the earth as solid mass, liquid mass, gases, and heat, the laws of nature are the principles by which those powers interact.

There is much we understand about nature, and much we do not understand. The study of physics is the study of nature's laws such as mechanics, acoustics, heat, and electricity. Throughout history, discoveries have been made about the laws of nature. Understanding the laws of nature has led to many technological advances that have changed how we live.

One law of nature that is critical in relation to the American dream is the law of thermodynamics. In part, this law holds that energy cannot be created or destroyed. Energy can only be transferred from a usable state to a nonusable state. Essentially, this law says that everything in nature is in a fixed or permanent state. How we as "one people" live in harmony with the laws of nature determines our quality of life and our ability to share in the American dream.

"AND NATURE'S GOD ENTITLE THEM …" This is the only use of the word "God" in either the Declaration of Independence or the Constitution of the United States. The Declaration of Independence makes no attempt to define "God." As matter of fact, I feel it safe to say that one of the most appealing aspects to the American dream is that the Constitution ensures the religious freedom to define "God" any way that one chooses.

Historically, most cultures believed in some type of spiritual being. Those spiritual beliefs led to a morale code that defined right and wrong. The author of the Declaration of Independence must have believed in a spiritual being. However, he offered no further reference to what is meant by "Nature's God."

What is meant by "Nature's God"? An important insight into how Thomas Jefferson viewed God can be seen in a letter he wrote to his nephew Peter Carr, whose parents were dead. Jefferson urged his nephew to scrutinize his belief in God with an open yet thoughtful mind, and accept it or reject it on his own terms. Faith, like other virtues, should be part of a self-examined life.

In that letter, Jefferson wrote, "He who made us would have been a pitiful bungler, if he had made the rules of our moral conduct a matter of science. For one man of science, there are thousands who are not. What would have become of them? Man was destined for society. His morality, therefore, was to be formed to this object. He was endowed with a sense of right and wrong, merely relative to this. The moral sense, or conscience, is as much a part of man as his leg or arm. It is given to all human beings in a stronger or weaker degree, as force of members is given them in greater or lesser degree. It may be strengthened by exercise, as may any particular limb of the body. This sense is submitted, indeed, in some degree, to the guidance of reason; but it is a small stock which is required for this: even a less one than what we call common sense."

Jefferson encouraged his nephew to search for God in his own way. He further stated, "Do not be frightened from this inquiry by any fear of its consequences. If it ends in a belief that there is no God, you will find incitements to virtue in the comfort and pleasantness you feel in its exercise, and the love of others which it will procure you. If you find reason to believe there is a God, a consciousness that you are acting under his eye, and that he approves you, will be a vast additional incitement; if that there be a future state, the hope of a happy existence in that increases the appetite to deserve it; if that Jesus was also a God, you will be comforted by a belief of his aid and love."

Jefferson concluded by saying, "In fine, I repeat, you must lay aside all prejudice on both sides, and neither believe nor reject anything, because any other persons, or description of persons, have rejected it or believed it. Your own reason is the only oracle given you by heaven, and you are answerable, not for the rightness, but uprightness of the decision."

One of the pillars that the American dream was built on is the right to define God any way an individual chooses to (or not believe in a God at all). We can do so without any government interference. It is clear that Jefferson had no intention of defining God but only suggested that one might find some comfort in the belief of a God; however, it is not necessary for a person to believe in a God to find happiness or peace of mind.

The word "entitled" is also an important part of the American dream. The literal definition of "entitled" is to give a legal right to. This means that all of us are "entitled" to the rights outlined in the Declaration of Independence and the Constitution of the United States. They are given to us by "Nature's God." No one has to earn these rights! They are a free gift, bestowed on us at birth, and can never be taken away from us.

"A decent respect to the opinions of mankind requires that they should declare the causes which impel them to the separation."

Each individual has a legal and moral right to have opinions. Those opinions are to be treated with a "decent respect." "Decent" means with honor and dignity. "Respect" means a high or special regard. "Opinions" are beliefs not based on absolute certainty or positive knowledge but on what seems true, valid, or probable to one's own mind or judgment. One does not have to be an expert to have an opinion.

Every person is "entitled by Nature's God" to have their opinions treated with respect. In order to share in the American dream, one must be treated with respect. Respect does not have to be earned! Each one of us is *entitled* to be treated with respect by our very nature. The very idea that someone must earn respect is to deny the rights given to us by the Declaration of Independence and the Constitution.

The first paragraph of the Declaration of Independence establishes our legal and moral right to the American dream as "one people." The American dream derives its powers from the earth and is guided by nature and Nature's God, which *entitle* us to be treated with respect and decency. We are separate entities but have equal stations in life. When, in the course of human events, things happen that undermine our legal and moral rights to which we are entitled, we are told by the Declaration of independence that we should "DECLARE THE CAUSES WHICH IMPEL THEM TO THE SEPARATION." We have the right to separate ourselves from those conditions that undermine our natural rights to participate in the American dream.

If there were any questions as to each person's absolute right to participate in the American dream, these words should put to rest any such doubts. "We" being one people—previously defined as an assemblage of people in large numbers associated in an agreement with respect to justice and a partnership for the common good—"We hold these truths" means that whatever follows these words cannot be disputed. The truth is the body of real things, events, and facts. When something is true, it cannot be disputed. The truth is beyond question. One of the things that makes the American dream so powerful is that it is based on the "TRUTH."

Tossed in for good measure, so there can be no doubt as to the meaning of the rights guaranteed us in the Declaration of Independence and the "separate and equal station" that each one of us is entitled to, the word "self-evident" leaves no doubt or confusion. Not only is the American dream based on the Truth, it is "SELF-EVIDENT"!

"THAT ALL MEN ARE CREATED EQUAL ..."

The American dream would hold little appeal or meaning if it were not for these words. What makes the American dream so magical is that it includes all of us as "one people." In order for the American dream to have any meaning at all, each person, regardless of race, gender, age, creed, any other characteristic, must have equal access to the dream.

I think it is safe to say that no other words in the Declaration of Independence have been more controversial or divisive than the words "CREATED EQUAL." It is historically accurate that at the time the Declaration was written, it was talking about white, land-owning adult males. People of color, women, and poor white males were not included or considered equal. They did not have the right to vote or participate in government. In the case of slaves, they had no rights whatsoever.

However, it is important to look at the time period during which the words "created equal" were written. Europe was being ruled by an aristocratic few, and there was no pretense of equality. By merely stating that "all men are created equal," Jefferson was changing the course of history. He was setting in motion one of the basic principles by which the dream was born, a principle to build a new society upon. He must have understood that in the world where he lived, all people were not treated equally. That is why he wrote the Declaration of Independence. The phrase, "ALL MEN ARE CREATED EQUAL," was not necessary for the American Revolution but was something to consider once the revolution was successful. What is clear by these words is that Jefferson had no intention of displacing one despotic ruler with another. He was looking toward a future world based on new principles.

This point can be more clearly understood when Abraham Lincoln was confronted by Senator Stephen Douglas in a debate over the Supreme Court's Dred Scott decision. Dred Scott, who was born a slave in Montana, filed suit on the grounds that temporary residence in a territory in which slavery was banned under the Missouri Compromise had made him free.

The majority opinion of the US Supreme Court, read by Chief Justice Taney, held that Scott, as an African Negro, could never be a citizen of any state, and therefore could not sue his owner in federal court.

Lincoln argued that the language of the Declaration should be interpreted as including all human beings without regard to sex or color or other traits that distinguish one human being from another. He made this point in Springfield, Illinois, by asserting that when it is understood that all human beings are equal not only in their common humanity but also in having by virtue of their common humanity the same human rights, it should not be concluded that the signers of the Declaration meant "the obvious untruth that all were then actually enjoying that equality, nor yet that they were about to confer it immediately upon them. In fact, they did not have the power to confer such a boon. They meant simply to declare the right, so that the enforcement of it might follow as fast as circumstances should permit."

The acceptance of the fact that all human beings are equal is an essential element in the American dream. The question then becomes, in what way are human beings equal? After all, no two human beings are exactly the same. Some of us are taller, smarter, faster, of different races and sexes. Each human being is different. Each human being is a complete and different entity unto himself or herself. It is not logical to think of human beings as being equal when compared to each other. No two human beings are exactly alike; therefore, no two human beings could be considered equal.

The only way human beings can be considered equal is to look at the whole. We are all part of one race, the human race. When one looks at a beautiful, lush, green lawn, we do not see each individual blade of grass. We do not think of any blade of grass as more valuable in relation to each other. Each blade of grass is unique and, when compared to each other, very different. Some would be stronger; some would be taller or shorter; no two would be exactly alike. When we look out at all those individual blades of grass, what we see is a lawn.

Only when viewed as a whole could human beings be considered equal. We are equal in that each human being is a part of the human race. Just as no single blade of grass could be said to be more valuable to a lawn, no human being could be said to be more valuable to the human race. We are all interconnected in our humanness.

All human beings are equal in the human race, the human species, *Homo sapiens*. When all human beings are seen as belonging to one race, they become equal in sharing the "powers of the earth."

When humans are divided into subgroups, the concept of being equal becomes diluted. When the Declaration was written, the prevalent belief was that the white race was superior to all other races. This belief allowed the institution of slavery to be morally justified, in that if one race is naturally superior to another, that race would have the right to control and dominate the inferior race. This is the basis for racism. As of this writing, the people of the United States have not resolved the issue of race.

The belief in racism allows for all kinds of behavior that, when viewed objectively, would be considered diabolical. With the belief that one race is superior to another, the survival of the fittest (or social Darwinism) permitted evil, barbaric behavior on behalf of the superior race.

Virtually all indigenous people from the Americas and other parts of the world have been decimated by racism. Racism and equality are polar opposites. One cannot believe in the American dream and accept racism. Not until all human beings are treated equally can the American dream truly exist.

It is important to note that there are other human beings who are not treated equally. Women, people with alternative sexual preferences, and young people are limited in their access to the American dream. Every human being is "ENTITLED" to share in the "POWERS OF THE EARTH" by "NATURE, AND NATURE'S GOD." This cannot be denied.

"They," meaning every human being, as "ONE PEOPLE." A collective of individuals making up the whole. The word "they" is significant in that it is generic. It does not specify a race, sex, or creed. The word "we" would also apply in this case. All of us.

We hold these truths to be self-evident. We all have the same nature. We all need to be loved; we all need to be needed. We are social beings. We are separate but interconnected. We are different but yet the same. All people have the same basic needs: nutritious food to eat, a safe shelter to live in that protects us from the elements, a healthy environment. This is the essence of the dream. Each word of the Declaration of Independence gives us the right to all the things that are essential to life. We also have the right to respect for the differences that we may have and the things we hold in common.

We are "endowed by our Creator." To be endowed something means provided for. It is given without having to earn it. It is every human being's inalienable right. These rights are absolute and given to us by our Creator. They are a free gift for simply being born into the human race!

The use of the word "Creator" is significant. This word can be interpreted many different ways. It is generic, in that it does not reference any specific religion. A person does not have to even believe in a Creator, because these rights are endowed upon all human beings without exception.

The Declaration of Independence does not say endowed by Jesus Christ, or by Mohammad, or by Buddha, or by any other religious leader. The word "their" is also important, in that it reinforces the idea that it is up to each person to define their "Creator" for themselves. If Jefferson had wanted to reference any religious being or specific religious group, he would have. If this was his intent, the Declaration of Independence would say "endowed by Jesus Christ." The use of the word "their" excludes any specific religious sect, because if the Declaration had said "endowed by Jesus Christ," a person who did not believe in Jesus Christ would be excluded from these rights. That was obviously not the intent of the Declaration of Independence.

"With certain inalienable rights ..."

It appears that Jefferson wanted to be very clear and leave absolutely no doubt that the Declaration of Independence includes every human being and cannot be questioned or denied. The rights that make up the American dream are divine rights, endowed by "their Creator." These are rights that transcend human laws. It does not matter what type of government is established, the rights established in the Declaration of Independence cannot be denied or taken away from us. Governments can enact laws that restrict our freedom; however, this does not take away our inalienable rights.

"Inalienable" means incapable of being surrendered or transferred. Human experience has shown that humans make laws restricting the rights of certain groups of people. Laws that discriminate, by their nature, reduce the rights of one group in favor of another. It could be said that is why the Declaration of Independence was written to begin with. The American Revolution was a result of people's rights being denied.

"That among these (rights) are Life, Liberty, and the Pursuit of Happiness."

These rights are at the core of the American dream. Every human being has the divine right to LIFE, LIBERTY, AND THE PURSUIT OF HAPPINESS. What else could anyone ask for? Doesn't everyone want to be happy? It is also true that one must be alive and free to pursue happiness.

The important word in this sentence is "among." It is the second time this word is used in the Declaration of Independence. The first time was in the phrase "AMONG THE POWERS OF THE EARTH." The word "among" is used in much the same way, in that it means a part of or more than one. It carries a slightly different meaning in this context. First, there are many natural laws and rights that are endowed to us by our Creator. Among all of these rights, but not exclusive to them, is the right to life.

"Life" is a very complex word. In part, it is the sequence of the physical and mental experiences that make up the existence of an individual. At the moment we are born, we are endowed by our Creator with the inalienable right to that life. When a child is born, he or she is totally dependent on its environment for its survival. Each person has a natural right to survive. This right must be given to all, equally and without question. A person's rights begin at birth and are mandated by their Creator.

If life is a person's experiences, both on a physical and a mental level, then it would follow that the moment we are born, our natural rights become our birthright. The physical world in which we live determines to a large extent what happens to us. Each person has an inalienable right to live in an environment that promotes life. We are entitled to all share in the "powers of the earth" that are a prerequisite to life.

Life is also for the duration of our earthly existence. From the moment we are born until the moment we die, we are guaranteed the inalienable rights to "LIFE, LIBERTY, AND THE PURSUIT OF HAPPINESS."

Not only do we have an inalienable right to life and all the inherent rights that go with life, we also have the right to do so with liberty! Liberty is another essential ingredient in the American dream. "Liberty" is a word that has tremendous power and many complexities. Without liberty, there would be no American dream.

Liberty means, in part, the quality or state of being free. To be free is the idea of not being dependent on others for one's survival. To be free is to be self-reliant. In the political sense, free means enjoying political independence from outside domination. To be free also means not determined by anything beyond its own nature or being.

Liberty also means freedom from arbitrary and despotic control. No one has the right to control us or deny us our divine right to have equal access to the powers of the earth. This goes to the very heart and soul of the American dream. It was the basis for the American Revolution. The American dream, in essence, is to be free. The earth has many powers, and as inhabitants of this earth, we have a right to share in those powers; no person has the right to deny our enjoyment of those powers.

Liberty also means the positive enjoyment of various social, political, or economic rights and privileges. "Positive" is another important dimension of the American dream. Not only do we have a right to life, we have a right to a positive life. We do that by enjoying a social position that enjoys all the privileges the earth can offer. We lead a positive life by enjoying political rights that guarantee us the right to share in those same privileges. Economic privileges are the production, distribution, and consumption of goods and services. We are endowed by our Creator to share in the things that are produced and the services that are offered.

Liberty, to a large extent, is dependent on how things are produced and distributed. In order for a person to live a positive life, they need to share in an adequate amount of the goods and services in the society in which they live.

Before the American dream, everything that was produced and all the services that were available were at the disposal of the hierarchy and granted to only a few. The ruling class determined how those goods and services were distributed. In this system, only the privileged few were allowed to share in the powers of the earth.

With the right to liberty, this was no longer true. Liberty is the power of choice. We each have the power of choice: the choice to choose how we live our lives. Unless the choice exists for all, it exists for none. The Declaration extends its blanket over all the people, not just a select few. If liberty was withheld from any person or group of people, it would not fulfill the mandate set forth in the Declaration of Independence.

Having inalienable rights to life and liberty creates unlimited potential in all of us. In essence, we each have the right to reach our full potential as a human being. We are guaranteed this right to live in a positive environment that facilitates that objective. We are *entitled* to these things. We don't have to earn them. To earn something means we have to do something to get those things, but these rights are inalienable, given to us by our Creator. We are not dependent on someone else to give us the goods and services that are necessary for a decent life. We do not have to earn the rights to life and liberty, because we are endowed by our Creator with these rights.

"AND THE PURSUIT OF HAPPINESS."

If the American dream could be summed up in one word, that word would be "happiness." For the first time in the social evolution of humans, a government was being instituted to ensure the inalienable right to pursue happiness. These words are the most important words in the Declaration of Independence, because they set in motion all that is needed for us to purse the American dream. All other rights are secondary to the objective to being happy. All other natural rights, such as life, liberty, and equality, are a means to an end, that end being happiness.

One could say I need the right to life and the right to be free and the right to be equal in order to pursue happiness. It could not be said that one wants to be happy in order for him or her to have life, liberty, or equality. Happiness differs from all other rights, in that it is the objective of all other rights.

The right to life is a vehicle to the pursuit of happiness. If we did not have the right to a quality life, it would be very unlikely that we could be happy. The same is true for the right to liberty. Happiness is the objective of liberty. If we, as human beings, were not free to make choices about how we live our lives, and were forced to live in a manner dictated by others, happiness would be a very difficult objective to attain.

Every human being desires happiness for themselves and their loved ones; this is an irrefutable fact. No matter where you come from, your religion, political beliefs, sexual preferences, age, race, or whatever, we all want to be happy.

Happiness is a state of being. It is complete. It is the ultimate desire. We can desire health, wealth, knowledge, or any number of things, but all these things are in "the pursuit of happiness." Happiness is a complete good. All other desires are partial goods. No matter how much wealth we attain or knowledge we have, these are incomplete in and of themselves. They are parts that go into making up the ultimate objective of being happy. When happiness is achieved, it leaves nothing more to be desired, for it involves the possession of all the things necessary to be happy.

The question remains, what does it mean to be happy? What did Jefferson mean by the phrase "pursuit of happiness"? It is true that what makes one person happy may not make another person happy. This is especially true when happiness is defined in the psychological sense. This definition would hold that happiness is a feeling of contentment produced by the satisfaction we experience when we are able to fulfill whatever desire we happen to have at any given moment in time.

If we use this definition of happiness, there would be no restrictions on what a person may desire in any given moment. In order for someone to be happy in this context, whatever a person desired would be justified in their pursuit of happiness. It would not matter that was at the expense of another person's wants or desires. Using this definition of happiness, a person could desire to own all the powers of the earth and not allow others to share in those powers. It would not matter whether a person ought to desire the things they need for their happiness.

In trying to determine what Jefferson was attempting to accomplish with the phrase "pursuit of happiness," we should understand other thoughts on this subject.

Jefferson had to be aware of what others had to say on the subject of happiness. This included fellow statesman George Mason, who drafted the Virginia Declaration of Rights a month before the Declaration of Independence was written. The Virginia Declaration opened with the words "That all men are by nature equally free and independent and have certain inherent rights … namely, the enjoyment of life and liberty, with the means of acquiring and possessing property, and pursuing and obtaining happiness and safety."

Jefferson dropped the word "obtain" and kept the word "pursuit." If he had accepted the definition of happiness as a feeling of contentment produced by the satisfaction we experience when we are able to fulfill whatever desires we happen to have at any given moment, he would have left the word "obtain" in the Declaration. This is so because using this definition of happiness is obtainable.

Another possible definition of happiness is a whole life lived well because it is enriched by the possession of all the goods that a morally virtuous human being ought to desire. If we use this definition, we would have a situation in which one could not achieve happiness at any given moment during the course of one's life. This is self-evident in the phrase "whole life." A whole life would be from the time a person's life begins to the time that person's life ends. Life is the process described previously. At any given moment, a person can experience happiness. No matter what a person's overall life condition is at any given moment, they could be happy in that moment. Whenever a person has a desire filled, whenever a person obtains an object or possession that he or she has desired, happiness can result in that moment. This moment will not last indefinitely. A person may attain momentary happiness in the use of a drug. When a person in under the influence of the drug, it could be said that person feels happiness. However, once the effects of the drug wear off, the state of being happy disappears.

When happiness is viewed from the context of a whole life lived well, each virtuous person would have the necessary resources to live in a state of happiness. The word "virtuous" is very important in this definition. "Virtue" means moral excellence or goodness. A virtuous person is honest and pure.

Resources that would facilitate a whole life well lived would include such things as nutritious food, a comfortable shelter, a good education, and protective clothing. These are all things that would be needed in order for one to be able to pursue happiness.

There is a significant difference between wants and needs. We could want something that is harmful. We could never need something that is harmful. To want something is to not have something and to desire it. To need something is to depend on something for existence.

We could want food that is harmful to us. We could desire an excess of food beyond what is good for us. A want becomes a negative in our life when we want things that are harmful to us or want an excess of things that are good for us.

If we define "happiness" as having all of our wants fulfilled, this would not be possible to achieve. For example, a person may want to became a dictator and control others with absolute authority. In order for that person to be happy, others would have to be unhappy. If a person wanted to take someone else's life, in order for them to be happy, they would deprive that person of his or her inalienable right to life.

When happiness is defined by our wants rather than our needs, it becomes a competition. This is because one individual having their wants met often is in conflict with another's, thus depriving others the necessary resources to live a whole life well. Using this definition, no government could act fairly, because the wants of one group are in conflict with another's. Government would have to take sides, thus favoring one group over another.

When we use the definition of a whole life lived well with the necessary resources needed to make life worth living, we see the need for living in a culture of cooperation. The spirit of happiness would be one of cooperation, not competiveness. One's pursuit of happiness would not conflict with another's. If happiness is fulfilling one's wants, it would be attainable for only a select few. If happiness is fulfilling one's needs, it is achievable for all.

The qualities of morality and virtue are states that only the individual could achieve for himself or herself. No society or government could ever confer virtue. Morality and virtue are internal by their nature. However, it is within the power of society to provide the external resources necessary in the pursuit of happiness. A government can only facilitate the pursuit of happiness; a government cannot ensure happiness.

"That to secure these rights, governments are instituted among men, deriving their just powers from the consent of the governed."

The American dream has such wide appeal because every person has the inalienable right to create the dream into reality. In order for people to create their dreams into reality, they must first know what it is they want to create. The Declaration of Independence was not the vehicle necessary to ensure the American dream. A government was necessary to "secure these rights."

It is clear that the type of society the Declaration of independence was envisioning was a world of equality, of liberty, where each person could pursue happiness. It was a world built upon the "powers of the earth" in relation to nature and Nature's God. The American dream was given to us by our Creator, who endowed us the right to it. What a wonderful dream. It is a world definitely worth believing in.

The Declaration of Independence also makes it clear that in order to secure the dream, a government must be instituted. The government's function is to safeguard the rights to life, liberty, and the pursuit of happiness for each one of us, as "ONE PEOPLE."

"Government" by definition is the organization, machinery, or agency through which people exercise authority; the United States government gets its authority from the consent of each one of us. Each person has been endowed by their Creator to the absolute undeniable rights to life, liberty, and the pursuit of happiness. Those are the rules, and the government's job is to facilitate those rules for each person.

Government's role is like that of a referee in a sporting event: acting to enforce the rules in a just, impartial manner. Ensuring justice is a primary responsibility of a government. In order for the American dream to have any basis in reality, the government must ensure that *everyone's* rights are protected fairly and equally.

It is the government's mandate to secure the rights given to us by our Creator. To "secure" something means to put it beyond hazard of losing. The government exists to ensure each person's access to the American dream.

"WHENEVER ANY FORM OF GOVERNMENT BECOMES DESTRUCTIVE OF THESE ENDS (life, liberty, and the pursuit of happiness) IT IS THE RIGHT OF THE PEOPLE TO ALTER OR TO ABOLISH IT, AND INSTITUTE NEW GOVERNMENT, LAYING ITS FOUNDATION ON SUCH PRINCIPLES, AND ORGANIZING ITS POWERS IN SUCH FORM, AS TO THEM SHALL SEEM MOST LIKELY TO EFFECT THEIR SAFETY AND HAPPINESS."

The Declaration of Independence is quite clear in defining what rights we are entitled to. In order to secure these rights, we collectively create a government that is mandated to ensure that we abide by nature and its laws, that each one of us has equal access to the powers of the earth in our pursuit of happiness.

However, if things ever go awry and large segments of the population are treated unjustly or if the powers of the earth are not shared in an equitable manner, we can rid ourselves of that government and replace it with a government that is "most likely to secure our safety and happiness." For the first time in human existence, a government was being created that derived its just powers from the consent of the people.

A unique aspect of the Declaration of Independence was that it put in place a procedure to be followed in the event that the government failed to live up to its responsibilities. If the government became destructive to our basic rights, we had the right (in fact, the duty) to alter or abolish it.

This was a very radical departure from past history. The American dream was created through a violent revolution. The Declaration of Independence was a repudiation of a government that was controlled by a very small minority with little concern for the rights of the vast majority—a government that was destructive to the ends of life, liberty, and the pursuit of happiness for the majority of people under its jurisdiction. The despotic rule of the king was antithetical to the objectives of the Declaration of Independence. The king had the absolute power to rule as he saw fit.

The Declaration of Independence was a rejection of this type of government and nurtured the belief that human beings were capable of running their own lives and being in control of their own fate. This was much more than a revolution against a political system. It was also a revolution against an economic system. The American dream relies as much on economic freedom as it does political freedom. Implicit in the Declaration of Independence is the recognition that in order for people to pursue happiness, they not only required political rights, they also required economic rights. Political rights and economic rights were equal partners in the "PURSUIT OF HAPPINESS."

Theodore Roosevelt reinforced this idea when he stated, "No man can be a good citizen unless he has a wage more than sufficient to cover the bare cost of living and hours of labor short enough so that after his day's work is done he will have time and energy to bear his share in the management of the community, to help in carrying the general load. We keep countless men from being good citizens by the conditions of life with which we surround them." Roosevelt recognized the importance of the need for a person to have some economic stability in order to pursue happiness.

The right to the American dream exists for all of us and those rights are supposed to be protected by the government. The government's role is to promote a system necessary for the fulfillment of the American dream. In order to have a realistic chance at being happy, we must have an adequate share of the available resources that are required for happiness. When we are denied access to the "powers of the earth," our political freedom is of little importance. If we cannot exercise our political freedoms because we are so bound by an economic system, we have the right to alter or abolish that system and replace it with a system that is most likely to effect our safety and happiness.

It seems quite simple. Government's role is to promote each person's safety and happiness. If the government fails to promote our safety and happiness, it becomes our responsibility to alter or abolish that government and replace it with a government that is more likely to do so.

To be truly safe, a person needs to live in a healthy environment and be free from harm or risk of death or injury. Safety allows that each person is secure from the threat of danger or serious loss. It is government's job to promote a safe environment for all of us in order for us to pursue happiness.

This does not mean that any time someone is unhappy, they should alter or abolish the government. The Declaration of Independence tells us, "Prudence, indeed, will dictate that governments long established should not be changed for light and transient causes; and accordingly all experience hath shown, that mankind are more disposed to suffer, while evils are sufferable, than to right themselves by abolishing the forms to which they are accustomed."

The idea that people will suffer, as long as evils are sufferable, can be applied to each one of us as well as all of us collectively, as in "one people." We humans have demonstrated a tremendous tolerance for pain and suffering. We seem to accomplish this by denying our true feeling and ignoring the conditions surrounding us.

To suffer is to be forced to submit to and endure something that is unpleasant or unfair. We can only continue to suffer as long as we continue to deny our suffering. We accept suffering as part of life. We endure suffering by telling ourselves such things as, "Nobody ever said life is fair" or "It's a dog-eat-dog world" or "It's a real rat race out there." These and a million other things are what we say to ourselves that help us accept suffering as a fact of life.

We suffer as long as "evils are sufferable." Denial also allows us to accept evil as a fact of life. Evil can be said to be anything that brings sorrow, distress, or calamity to our lives. To be evil is to have bad character or behave in a destructive manner. Evil is a moral wrong. We choose to overlook evil by convincing ourselves that things are not so bad.

For example, drug addicts or alcoholics deny that their behaviors are destructive; similarly, we collectively deny how our behaviors are destructive. A part of denial that permits destructive behavior is to compare one's condition to another's. We accept suffering by telling ourselves that our suffering is not as bad as someone else's suffering. Denial helps us find comfort in other people's suffering because we could always be worse off.

Denial helps us accept evil to a point. Once evil becomes intolerable, we must make the changes necessary to promote our happiness and safety. Only by breaking through denial and stopping our destructive behavior can we pursue happiness.

Not until we as "one people" decide we can no longer tolerate the evils in the world will any change take place. The Declaration of Independence was written at a time when people had decided that they had suffered enough. They enacted laws that they believed would most likely promote their safety and happiness.

The Declaration of Independence set forth the principles that created the American dream, the dream of living in a world where each person can share among the powers of the earth the necessary resources to live a whole life well, a world where each one of us is treated as an individual and recognizes that each of us enjoys an equal station, a world that is guided by the laws of nature and Nature's God, a world where each one of us is endowed by our Creator with the inalienable rights to life, liberty, and the pursuit of happiness.

The dream is to be safe and happy. When evil forces are destructive to the general safety and happiness of the people, it becomes necessary to defeat those forces and institute new guidelines that most likely will ensure our safety and happiness.

It seems quite clear that the Declaration of Independence intended to create a world in which the government, which gets its powers from the consent of the people, acts to ensure the absolute rights to life, liberty, and the pursuit of happiness for every man, woman, and child. The Declaration of Independence was written because those who set out to create a new society determined that the despotic rule they found themselves under was destructive toward the right of the people to life, liberty, and the pursuit of happiness. The Declaration of Independence listed several grievances against the despotic rule and institutions they believed were detrimental to their safety and happiness. The Declaration of Independence was a mission statement, and the Constitution was the mechanism by which a new government was to be based in order to fulfill that mission.

CHAPTER SIX

Not Safe or Healthy

THE WORLD HAS OBVIOUSLY changed greatly since the Declaration was written. We live in very different times. We are no longer an agriculturally based society where every person could carve a piece of the earth for themselves and become self-sufficient. Our world is suffering from high unemployment, pollution, war, crime, poor education, lack of sufficient health care, and many other maladies.

I believe that our government has failed to protect us and no longer represents the vast numbers of citizens that it is its duty to protect. The economic indicators are undeniable. The gap between the haves and have-nots is growing larger with each passing day. It is true that many citizens live in economic security and share in the bounty this economic and political system affords. It is also true that this number is dwindling with no relief in sight. The Declaration of Independence listed a number of grievances against the king of England and his despotic rule. I propose a new list of grievances against the current economic and political system that I believe no longer holds the interest of the average citizen in its purview. Those grievances are as follows:

The first grievance against the government is that it promotes an economic system that is based on the mass consumption of the powers of the earth. We have come to define ourselves as consumers. To consume something means to destroy or devour it. The government has followed an economic policy that determines its success by the amount of natural resources we consume as a society. Under this system, the more powers of the earth we consume, the better off we are supposed to be.

This economic policy has wreaked havoc on nature, created significant poverty, and in general undermined the spirit of the Declaration of Independence. In a consumer society, the powers of the earth are owned and controlled by a very small minority, who command huge profits from the consumption of those powers. In order for individuals to benefit from the powers of the earth, they must purchase what is rightfully theirs to begin with. To understand how the policies of the government have placed the powers of the earth in the hands of a small minority is to understand the history of the development of these policies.

There is no better example of how the promotion of mass consumption began than to look at the development of the lifeblood of the consumer society, the oil industry. Fossil fuels make up over 90 percent of the energy used to run the consumer society. Petroleum makes up about half of the energy requirements in our consumer society.

According to the *New American Encyclopedia*, petroleum is a naturally occurring mixture of hydrocarbons, usually found in liquid form or "crude oil." Petroleum is believed to be formed over millions of years from organic debris, chiefly plankton and simple plants. As these organic substances died, they were rapidly buried in sediment underwater, which stopped the oxidation process. As time went along and after some biodegradation, the earth's temperature changed and pressure built up, which caused cracks in the earth's surface. Over time, the rock holding the oil was compacted and the oil and moisture were forced out and slowly migrated into porous reservoir rocks, chiefly sandstone or limestone. Finally, a secondary migration occurred within the reservoir as the oil coagulated to form a pool. This pool was sealed by some type of covering. Natural gas was trapped within this covering. Some oil seeped to the earth's surface.

The first oil well was drilled in west Pennsylvania in 1859. Up until this time, only oil that seeped to the surface was available for any use. Once the industry could extract oil in large amounts, the consumer society began. The oil industry grew so fast that it now supplies over half of the world's energy as well as the materials for our consumer products.

Nature took millions of years to create oil. One of the goals of our consumer society is to suck as much oil out of the earth as we can and burn it. We do not care about the harmful effects gaining access to oil may cause. We do not care about the effects caused by turning oil into a poisonous gas. We care little when huge quantities of oil are spilled into our oceans, lakes, and rivers. No matter how we modify our consumer society, its goal will always be to consume and destroy the powers of the earth.

The objective of a consumer society is to destroy natural resources. Oil is a primary example of that. Once oil is extracted from the earth and burned for fuel, it is gone forever. It can never be replaced. No matter how much oil or other fossil fuels may exist on earth, eventually we will have sucked the last drop of oil from its hiding place and mined the last bit of coal. The goal of our consumer society is to devour as many natural resources as we can, as fast as we can.

Oil is just one example of how our consumer society destroys nature and its resources. A consumer society is dependent on many other natural resources such as exotic metals, water, timber, and land; these resources are all finite and cannot be replaced once they are used. Resources can only be transferred from a usable state to a nonusable state.

The race to consume natural resources dictates government policy. Our consumer society requires an endless supply of natural resources. The fact is that we do not have the necessary resources to fuel our need to consume. Therefore, we need to look elsewhere for those resources. In order to ensure that our supplies of resources flow continually, we need a powerful military to protect our way of life. Put another way, we need to protect our need to consume. The use of violence or the threat of violence is necessary for the consumer state's survival.

Our government's primary function has been to protect our consumer society and the large corporations that profit from that consumption. In doing so, it engages in both covert and overt military actions all over the world. The government has been in some type of military action since World War II, all to protect our way of life or our ability to consume.

The second grievance against the government is that it does not treat all people equally. The government promotes the interests of a few at the expense of the many. As a result of this policy, the powers of the earth are unequally distributed.

At the time the Declaration was written, it was clear that the ruling class was the king and those with royal blood. The purpose of the American Revolution was to replace a system of inequality with a system based on equality.

Under our present form of government, there are two groups of people: those who own the powers of the earth and those who must pay to share in those powers. This negates the mandate of the Declaration of Independence. Whether the powers of the earth are owned by those of royal blood or owned by a few wealthy individuals, the net effect is the same. A small minority dictates how the vast majority will live.

There are two separate but equally important elements in society that determine a person's access to the pursuit of happiness. There is the government, which is related to our political freedom, and the economy, which is related to how we make a living. Neither one could be said to be more important than the other in determining how we live our lives. Both play an equal role in the pursuit of happiness.

Our political institutions are ensured by the Declaration of Independence, the Constitution, and its amendments. Theoretically, every person has an equal say on how our government operates. Our political rights such as freedom of speech, freedom of religion, and the freedom of the press are all essential ingredients in our pursuit of happiness. Each one of us is guaranteed our rights in a political sense.

The economy is run on a very different set of rules. There are no guarantees when it comes to making a living. The consumer society has its roots in the philosophy of "every person for themselves." The people that control the resources determine how those resources will be distributed. It is fair to say that the more of the resources of the earth they control, the freer they are to pursue happiness.

While our economic system and political system are of equal importance in our pursuit of happiness, their nature is very different. Within our political system, we are all considered equal and have a say on how those institutions are run. This is not the case in the economic system. There is a clear understanding of our political rights because there is a document that clearly defines those rights. There is no such guideline for our economic institutions. Our economic system simply "evolved" into what it is today.

There was disagreement among the framers of the Constitution regarding who should be included in its protection. There were those who strongly believed that only people of "proper breeding" should be allowed protection and participation in the Constitution. This faction wanted to replace the aristocracy of Europe with an aristocracy of their own. They did not believe that all people were equal.

The other faction believed that the powers of the earth should be more evenly distributed. They held that more people should have a voice in their government and how things were done. Thomas Jefferson envisioned an agrarian society where people could enjoy freedom, in that they would own and control the resources necessary to live a whole life well. In this vision, Jefferson saw little need for government.

As these two viewpoints competed with each other, the economy continue to evolve. The country was quickly divided into three factions: the industrial North, the plantations of the South, and the small farmers and ranchers of the West. As time went on, the conflict between them grew more intense.

The South, with its large plantations, depended on slave labor to maintain profits and a regal lifestyle. The South also relied on low tariffs on imported goods so it could buy the necessary goods to run its estates at the lowest possible cost.

On the other side of this issue was the industrial North and agrarian system of the West. They believed that slavery provided an unfair advantage to the Southern plantations. This side was determined to keep taxes on imported goods high to protect their profits. Slavery and tariffs were economic issues that tore this country apart.

Both sides tried to work out their differences through the political arena. Great debates took place; compromises were tried but failed. In 1861, the country exploded into the bloodiest war in our history. Some six hundred thousand lives were lost but little was resolved.

The African people who were kidnapped from their homes, stripped of their humanity, and transported to the New World were not set free and treated as equals to share in life, liberty, and the pursuit of happiness. They were cut loose to fend for themselves. They were placed in a state of limbo, enjoying neither the rights of freedom nor the protection of slavery. One day they were slaves, and the next they were free. Racism did not magically disappear, nor did these "freed" people enjoy any economic benefits. In many ways, their condition became worse.

Since that time, other groups of people have been treated unequally; they do not share equally in the pursuit of happiness. Government policies, through laws and special interests, fail to resolve the issue of race.

The issue of race will never be resolved until we find a way to create a world that permits every human being to be treated equally and enjoy the rights to life, liberty, and most of all the pursuit of happiness.

The present government cannot resolve the issue of race because it is a tool of special interests. The only way a person can be elected to a position of power is to have the financial backing of the wealthy. Without being elected to office, there's no way to see that the powers of the earth were equitably distributed. The wealthy are invested in protecting their wealth. Government offices are bought, usually by the highest bidder. Running for government office has become a billion-dollar industry. People spend millions of dollars to be elected to offices that pay them only a fraction of that amount.

The present government is managed by two political parties that are dependent on the wealthy for their financing. Both protect the interest of the wealthy. They disagree only on how the powers of the earth should be distributed by the wealthy. The issue of how to share the powers of the earth equitably and promote happiness cannot be resolved by the present government, as long as those powers of the earth are owned by a small minority of greedy individuals.

The third grievance against the present government is that its policy of violence, through the buildup of the military industrial complex, is destructive to the goal of the American dream to be happy. It is a safe observation to say that we as "one people" promote violence.

Our nation was born through a violent revolution. Through a systematic policy of violence and deception, we all but annihilated the indigenous people who occupied the Americas long before this continent was "discovered." We also enslaved a whole race of people and then sacrificed hundreds of thousands of human beings to decide whether we should free them or not.

With the advent of the industrialization of violence, our ability to slaughter human beings reached unacceptable heights. The first war fought by industrialized nations was World War I. While the United States was still the "new kid on the block," we were eager to join in the wholesale slaughter of millions of human beings. Because weapons of destruction could be mass-produced, over 8.4 million men, women, and children were killed and maimed worldwide.

After the "War to End All Wars," the industrialized nations continued to develop new technologies that improved upon their ability to destroy human life. Not long after World War I, the sequel was unleashed: World War II. It was just like a movie sequel: all the main characters were back, with more spectacular weapons of mass destruction.

The government of the United States took the lead in developing weapons of mass destruction. We developed a weapon of such destructive force that we could literally destroy the world! World War II ended in spectacular fashion. We showed the world just what we were capable of. With two bombs, we destroyed two cities and killed over two hundred thousand men, women, and children. All totaled, over 30 million human beings were slaughtered during World War II.

After World War II, the United States became number one in mass destruction, and the government was determined to maintain its lead. Despite the warnings of the former leader of the Allied Forces and the president of the United States, Dwight D. Eisenhower, the government committed a substantial amount of the powers of the earth to the continued development of the military industrial complex.

The military has become an integral part of the fabric of our society. The military justifies its existence through the philosophy that in order to have peace, we must be prepared for war. The military has taken on the task of protecting our way of life (mass consumption) and our economic interests (to secure resources necessary to fuel mass consumption) all over the world. Our government has declared itself the "policemen" of the world and continues to devote a significant amount of our resources toward this policy of violence and military action.

The government flirted with the idea of making a sequel to World War II, but even the most violent, hawkish leaders realized that another unlimited war could mean the destruction of the world as we know it. So the question became how to flex our military might and continue devoting huge amounts of our resources to a policy of violence and terror.

So the idea of a cold war was born. The logic behind this war was simple: Since we cannot fight an unlimited war that would spell doom for all concerned, we decided to pretend we were at war. This logic worked perfectly. Since we were now fighting the Cold War, we could continue to spend billions of dollars on weapons of mass destruction, with the objective of never using them. Behind this philosophy, the military industrial complex grew by leaps and bounds.

The driving force behind a policy of violence is the need for an enemy. After Word War II, the world was divided into two opposing philosophies: capitalism (mass consumption) and communism.

These were perfect adversaries. Both sides hated each other with equal passion. The battle cry of "Better dead than Red" justified the continuation of the policy of violence and the buildup of the military industrial complex.

The Cold War had two leading characters: the United States and the Soviet Union. Both sides committed huge amounts of their resources to prepare for a war they both knew they could never fight.

An offshoot of the policy of violence and the Cold War was the development of the "limited war." While both sides accepted the fact that they could never risk another all-out shooting match, there was nothing to stop them from fighting a limited war.

At this time in history, the world was divided into two basic categories: the United States and its allies, and the Soviet Union and its allies. Attacking one of those countries would result in an all-out war. However, there were smaller, poorer countries that were fair game. These countries were referred to as the third world. It was acceptable under the rules of the Cold War to bomb the hell out of these people.

Under the policy of a limited war, a country could kill as many people as they liked as long as they were in the third world. The first of these limited wars was the Korean conflict (that is another aspect of limited wars: they were called conflicts, not wars). After World War II, Korea was divided into the Communist North and the capitalist South. A civil war broke out between the two Koreas. When it appeared that the North might defeat the South, the United States jumped in to protect its interest.

The conflict raged on and looked like it could grow to world war status, but cooler heads prevailed. So after hundreds of thousands of deaths and much suffering on both sides, this limited war was fought to a standstill. One thing that came out of this was that the government now knew that it could fight a limited war.

The Cold War dominated government policy, both domestically and internationally; at home the government pursued a type of witch hunt, looking for "Commies." The House Committee on Un-American Activities destroyed many lives, using the Cold War as their justification. Abroad, the military continued to act as the policemen of the world.

The Cold War heated up as both sides continued to develop huge armies and built an arsenal of nuclear weapons that ensured the destruction of mankind many times over. Things almost got out of hand during the Cuban Missile Crisis. Fortunately, the "enemy" backed down and catastrophe was averted.

The world situation remained tense, with both sides arming themselves to the hilt. It was only a matter of time before the government policy of violence would find a suitable situation to flex its muscles. Vietnam filled the bill. It fit the basic requirement for fighting a limited war. It was a third-world country, it was broken into two parts (the Communists of the North and the free South), and it was unlikely to lead to an unlimited war.

Once again, the policy of violence got to flex its muscles and fight a limited war. It was pretty close to the real thing. The military got to do all the things they would do in an unlimited war. They got to mobilize millions of nineteen-year-olds and ship them thousands of miles from their homes. They were able to use all their new technology and demonstrate their military might to the world.

Blowing up villagers in their grass huts or while they were tending their rice paddies was acceptable under the rules of limited warfare. We dropped more bombs on those grass huts, in that small third-world country, than all the bombs we used in World War II.

This was one heck of a limited war. The only drawback was that those villagers fought back with such ferocity that our losses became unacceptable, even for hawkish conservative Americans. After sacrificing some fifty-five thousand American soldiers (and, by some estimates, 3 million Vietnamese), we had enough. For the first time in our history, we lost!

The defeat did not discourage the government's policy of violence. We may have lost the battle, but we were determined to win the war. Even though the military got its nose bloodied during the Vietnam conflict, they used the loss to underscore the need for newer weapons and more technologies. The policy of violence continued, but some began to question its validity.

After the Vietnam conflict, the American people were losing their taste for blood. The policy of violence had lost some of its steam. When all those soldiers came back from Vietnam, the economy was in the dumps and millions of people were out of work. Things looked pretty bleak when, just like an old Western, Ronald Reagan came to town to save the day.

Reagan decided to pursue the policy of violence with a vengeance and stepped up the rhetoric against the "Evil Empire." He managed to whip up enough support to finance one of the largest military buildups in our history. He also managed to make the enemy believe that he was going build a "shield" around our country to protect us, leaving them defenseless. Reagan demonstrated to the world that we would commit any amount of our resources to ensure that our policy of violence would be successful. He did not seem to care how much money he had to borrow to follow such a policy.

The Soviet Union, realizing it could not devote the type of resources necessary to keep on fighting the Cold War, said uncle and gave up. This left a void that had to be filled in order to justify the continuation of the policy of violence. Not wasting any time, those who espoused the policy of violence found the perfect enemy: Saddam Hussein.

Saddam Hussein was the front man for a bigger enemy called "terrorists." Instead of communism, our enemy became terrorism.

Communism is a specific philosophy with specific goals—a very definable enemy. What the heck is a terrorist?

The next limited war after Vietnam was Iraq. We showed the world exactly what we got for all those billions of dollars we spent under Reagan. We "kicked Saddam's butt." The policy of violence finally had a winner. Saddam survived the first limited war, but 175,000 other Iraqi people did not.

After the first Iraqi conflict, the policy of violence again started to lose steam. But as fate would have it, on September 11, 2001, a group of men commandeered four jet planes and crashed two of them into the Twin Towers and another into the Pentagon. The fourth was taken back by passengers and crashed into an empty field. For the past ten-plus years, we have been at war with no end in sight.

I say that it's time to stop using our natural resources to pursue this insane policy of violence. I contend that the government's policy of violence is destructive to the pursuit of happiness; therefore, it must be abolished and replaced with a policy that will most likely effect our safety and happiness.

In conclusion, there are three policies that our government practices that are destructive of the pursuit of happiness:

1. The government promotes an economic system that is based on the mass consumption of the world's resources.
2. The government promotes policies under which people are not treated equally with equal opportunities to the pursuit of happiness.
3. The government practices a policy of violence.

The world can be anything we as "one people" want it to be. The present world we live in is nothing more than a collection of people's dreams. Our consumer-driven, industrialized, militaristic, profit-at-all-cost society is the result of individuals' dreams. Those individuals have managed to capture the powers of the earth and impose their will on the rest of us. This small minority accomplished this through an unjust use of power to dictate how we live our lives.

The definition of oppression is a condition under which a small minority dictates how the majority live their lives. Oppression is a destructive force in the pursuit of happiness. Oppression is the exact opposite of liberty. In an oppressive society, people have few choices on how they live their lives. Freedom is dependent on how many choices we can make regarding how we live our lives. The more choices available, the freer we are.

When a small group of people control the powers of the earth, they dictate how we can access those resources. Our choices are dependent on their rules. We either comply with those rules or suffer the consequences.

Each one of us chooses how we live our lives. Those choices determine who we become and what kind of society we live in. People choose those behaviors that reward them and avoid those behaviors that penalize them. We agree to live our lives a certain way in order to gain access to the resources necessary to pursue happiness.

We choose to purchase the consumer items required to live in today's society. We do so for many reasons. One is the motivation of being like everybody else. We all want to fit in. Our consumer goodies in many ways define us. We choose to buy certain vehicles. We choose to risk our lives every day and go to places we rather not be. We choose to work in jobs we really don't want because we need the paycheck. We choose to do these things because the perceived penalty is too great.

We accept that life isn't fair. We convince ourselves that things are not that bad. We compare ourselves to other cultures, finding comfort in other people's misery. Somehow it makes us feel better that there are people in the world who are far worse off than we are.

Many of us have become fatalistic. We believe things will never change. We have convinced ourselves that this is the way the world is and we just have to make the best of it. We choose to accept the rules of the society we live in.

We could choose to create a world where people live in harmony with nature—a world where people are free from hunger and disease; not a utopia, but a world that is not built on violence and destruction of our natural resources, a place where children can be children, a place where we take care of the sick, a place where a person can grow old with dignity and know they will never be tossed out in the streets. We can choose to live in any kind of world we want. We could choose to establish new rules based on new principles that are most likely to ensure our safety and happiness.

CHAPTER SEVEN

American Dream Revisited

In order to create a gentler, kinder society, there need to be some major paradigm shifts. I am proposing five new principles to ensure our safety and happiness:

First Principle: Replace Mass Consumption with Conservationism

The economy needs to change from a consumer society to a conservationist society.

Instead of judging our society's success by how much we consume, our success would be determined by how much we save. The principle of conservation would be the opposite of the way we live in today's economy. In the consumer society, waste is good. The more people throw away, the better the economy does. In order for a consumer society to be doing well, people must constantly buy products that they consume in a short amount of time or throw away. Consumer products are made not to last so we can toss them in the garbage and buy new products, in a never-ending cycle. In a consumer society, the higher we pile the garbage, the more successful we consider ourselves.

The goal of an economy based on conservation would be to save the powers of the earth, our natural resources, for future generations and use only those resources necessary for all of us to live a whole life well. To conserve something means to keep it from being damaged, lost, or wasted. In a conservationist economy, it would be the responsibility of each generation to preserve the powers of the earth for future generations.

The principle of conservation is based on the belief that there is an abundance of the powers of the earth for everyone to live a whole life well. In a conservationist society, the earth's resources would be used in conjunction with the laws of nature and Nature's God. They would be distributed in a way that is most likely to ensure a person's safety and happiness.

Instead of looking at the powers of the earth as something to be consumed, they would be treated as something to be loved and nurtured. In a conservationist economy, the earth's resources would be protected. An economy based on the principle of conservationism accepts the old adage, "Waste not, want not."

In the present consumer economy, technology is used to find new ways to consume the earth's resources. Millions of people are employed to develop new ways to consume these resources. Consumer products eventually become landfill in the never-ending process of consumption. Bright and talented people are developing new technologies to produce consumer items such as chewing gum, soda pop, frozen dinners, and thousands of other products. The goal of these consumer products is to produce things that we "want" but don't actually need.

In a conservationist economy, all of those bright minds that are being used to produce useless consumer items would be redirected toward the gold of building the safest, healthiest environment possible. The powers of the earth are enormous and plentiful. The goal of the conservationist economy would be to use technology to provide all the things that are necessary for a life well lived for the entire population.

A conservationist economy would use technology to draw upon the renewable powers of the earth. It stands to reason that if all the energy and technology that is being used in the development of consumer goods and weapons of mass destruction were refocused on creating a healthy environment, we could create the kind of world we want to live in. It's just a matter of choice, not ability. If we can walk on the moon, we can feed everybody on the earth. If we can figure out a way to destroy all living things, we can figure out a way to preserve life. It's a matter of choice.

The goal of a conservationist economy would be to use the powers of the earth to provide the essentials of life such as good food, safe shelter, and meaningful work for all people.

The focus of the consumer economy is to create wealth. The focus of the conservationist economy is to create health. The definition of wealth is accumulating money or material goods. The goal of wealth is to acquire material objects beyond what any one person could possibly use. The goal of health is to provide for a person's physical and mental well-being.

In a consumer society, a person can accumulate and consume material goods without limits. They can do so without regard to the harmful effects such consumption has on their health or the health of the environment. It is a law of nature that when a person consumes more of any substance than they need, that substance becomes harmful to them. Conservationism holds that too much of anything is harmful and unhealthy, therefore a destructive force in the pursuit of happiness.

A society based on conservationism would work in harmony with nature and its laws. Our communities would be built to optimize the use of the powers of the earth. We would design communities so they would work in harmony with the environment.

The laws of nature tell us that there is an optimum size to all things. Once things grow beyond their optimum size, they become unhealthy and dysfunctional. This holds true for individuals as well as businesses and governments. The goal of creating an economy based on conservation would be to harmonize with this law and build communities in a way that would work with the powers of the earth.

We have two choices: either we continue to choose to live in a society based on mass consumption, or we choose to live in a society based on conservationism.

SECOND PRINCIPLE: ALL HUMAN BEINGS ARE CREATED EQUAL

The second principle that is most likely to effect our safety and happiness is that all human beings are of equal value and therefore are entitled to their fair share of the powers of the earth. A society that encompasses this principle also recognizes the importance of all of the Creator's creations as they relate to the pursuit of happiness.

Respect for life is the cornerstone of the second principle. In order for every human being to be truly equal, each person must be treated with respect. To be respected means that everyone would be held in high regard and valued for their uniqueness. Each individual would be given the utmost consideration in the pursuit of happiness.

Equality is a necessary condition in the pursuit of happiness, because as long as there are individuals or groups of people that are limited in their access to the powers of the earth, we all suffer.

Poverty breeds disease. Poverty means not having the resources necessary to live a healthy life. When people are denied access to the resources essential to life, they become desperate. Desperate people do desperate things.

The inequitable distribution of the earth's resources is the cause of much of the suffering in the world today. As long as there are individuals that accumulate large quantities of the world's resources and other individuals who have no resources, none of us can be truly happy. This is because one person's happiness would come at the expense of another.

THIRD PRINCIPLE: ROOSEVELT'S ECONOMIC BILL OF RIGHTS

The third principle that would be necessary to ensure the absolute right to the pursuit of happiness is a new economic Bill of Rights. In 1944 President Roosevelt addressed the Congress and asserted that true freedom could not exist without economic freedom; he proposed the following economic rights:

1. All people have the right to meaningful work.
2. All people have the right to adequate food to sustain a healthy life.
3. All businesses have the right to trade in an atmosphere of freedom from unfair competition.
4. All people have the right to live in a decent home.
5. All people have the right to adequate medical care and the opportunity to achieve and enjoy good health.
6. All people have the right to live a whole life well.
7. All people have the right to a good education.

The first item reflects the basic human need to feel that one is contributing something to the whole. We are social beings. Each one of us has a special talent and something different to offer. People cannot be happy unless they have the means to express their uniqueness.

While the powers of the earth are plentiful, we must harness those powers in a way that will allow each of us to live a healthy, meaningful life. The process of turning the resources the earth provides into the goods necessary to live is work. Work in a consumer economy has been translated into making money. Work in a conservationist economy means that whatever a person contributes according to his or her own ability is sufficient to earn that person the necessary resources to live a whole life well.

The second item in the economic Bill of Rights is based on the belief that no person should go without adequate resources to be safe and happy. That is not to say that every person must have the exact same amount of resources. Those who work harder or contribute more to the whole deserve to be rewarded for those efforts. However, it is the unjust accumulation of the earth's resources by a few individuals that is inherently unfair. It is unjust when the powers of the earth are enjoyed in excess by a few when at the same time large numbers of people can barely extract enough resources to survive.

The second right does not mean that people should be given those resources without some type of contribution. It takes work to extract the necessary resources to live a whole life well. In a conservationist economy, goods would not be mass-produced in factories that require huge amounts of fossil fuels. Instead, new methods of production, relying on renewable energy such as human energy, will be developed, making human beings more valuable than machines.

The third right is based on the belief that all one must do to share in the powers of the earth is contribute something. In the present consumer economy, businesses are in competition with each other. Businesses consolidate to gain an advantage over their competition in order to increase their profits. In a conservationist economy, people would be working together in harmony with nature to provide the safest, healthiest environment possible.

The fourth right is not just referring to the physical structure in which one lives but the surrounding community as well. In a conservationist economy, communities would be built to maximize the renewable energy available. People would live close to food sources, recreation, and their work. Homes would be built to allow for privacy and individual taste.

The fifth right, to adequate health care, is based on the belief that everyone has the right to live in a healthy environment—an environment that is created in relation to the powers of the earth and the laws of nature, an environment that most likely allows for our safety and happiness.

Medical science's goal is to identify any biological or psychological forces that are destructive in achieving good health and continued enjoyment of that good health. Once identified, those forces would be minimized (if not eliminated entirely). The fifth right is based on the further belief that we have the capacity to create a healthy environment for every person. All we have to do is choose to do so. Nature provides everything necessary to live a whole life well for each and every one of us.

The sixth right is based on the belief that from the moment of birth to the moment our spirit leaves our body, we have the absolute right to share in the resources necessary for life, liberty, and the pursuit of happiness. These rights are guaranteed to us by our Creator and cannot be denied.

In a world based on the sixth right, every child will be welcomed with open arms from birth. While each of us has biological parents, it will be the responsibility of the community to ensure that each child has the adequate resources to be safe and happy.

The sixth right guarantees that through a person's entire life, no matter if they become ill or meet with some type of incapacitating accident, they will be taken care of. It is the obligation of the healthy to care for those less fortunate.

The sixth right is also based on the belief that as a person grows older, his or her knowledge and wisdom increase. In a world based on the sixth principle, old age would not be something to fear but something to enjoy.

The seventh and final economic right is based on the belief that in order for each of us to share adequately in the powers of the earth, we must have the tools necessary to do so. It is the purpose of education to provide these tools.

The purpose of education is to aid in the development of everyone's mind, body, and spirit, which will prepare them to reach their fullest potential. There is much to be done in creating a healthy, safe environment, and every human being is vital in this task.

Since each individual is unique, we each have something different to contribute to the welfare of the whole. Some of us have an aptitude for building things; some of us are more gifted in the arts; some of us have more ability in math and the sciences. There are an infinite number of ways that each of us can contribute to the happiness of the whole. The purpose of education is to help each of us find that gift and develop it to our fullest potential.

FOURTH PRINCIPLE: THE GOVERNMENT MUST SECURE PEACE AT HOME AND ABROAD

The fourth principle that the conservationist economy would be based on is that a primary function of government is to secure peace, both domestically and externally. To live in a state of peace means to be in harmony with one's environment. It also means to live without the threat of war or internal conflict. It is our right to live in a world free of hostilities.

In a world based on this principle, the only justification for violence would be to defend oneself. Self-defense means that there is a direct threat or use of violence against an individual, a group of people, or a nation. Violence can only be used as an absolute last resort.

All weapons of mass destruction would be eliminated, and all research regarding their development would be halted. There would no longer be a professional armed force, and troops would be brought home from around the world. All the resources that are currently used to produce greater weapons of violence and maintain an armed force would be used to resolve conflicts through peaceful means.

FIFTH PRINCIPLE: THE SPIRIT OF COOPERATION

The fifth and final principle a conservationist society would be based on is the spirit of cooperation. To cooperate means to act or work together for a common purpose. The common purpose that each of us will be working toward is the safety and happiness of all human beings. In a world based on this principle, people will no longer be in competition with each for the powers of the earth.

This principle is also based on the belief that people all over the earth are interconnected. In a world based on this principle, the emphasis would be placed on what all humans have in common rather than how they are different. It is also based on the belief that all human beings have the same needs and the powers of the earth are ample in meeting those needs. Only by working together in the spirit of cooperation can each of us have our needs met.

In conclusion, here are the five principles the new dream would be based on:

1. Mass consumption would be replaced by conservationism.
2. All human beings are created equal.
3. An economic Bill of Rights.

4. The government must secure peace at home and abroad.
5. The spirit of cooperation.

CHAPTER EIGHT

A Dream

I AWOKE FROM A deep sleep. As I wiped the sleep from my eyes, a sense of panic flooded over my body. I had no idea where I was. My surroundings were completely unfamiliar to me. I leaped out of bed, my heart pounding a million miles a minute. My mind began to race. Where was I? How did I get here?

I stood there shaking, trying to clear my mind. I told myself to get a grip. I took a deep breath and reasoned that there must be a logical explanation for my present predicament. I sat down on the bed and tried to remember what I was doing before I fell asleep. The last thing I could remember was a light shining so brightly that it hurt my eyes. I couldn't remember anything prior to the light. It seemed that all other memory had been wiped from my mind. My next thought was that I must still be asleep. I pinched my arm to check this theory. I must have had a lot of adrenaline pumping through my body, because that pinch really hurt.

The pain from the pinch took my mind off my situation. As I rubbed my self-inflicted wound, I looked around the room. A sense of calm replaced the panic I was feeling. I was in a bedroom, but it was unlike any room I had ever seen before. The bed was large but not too large. The wooden bedposts appeared to be hand carved. An intricate comforter lay atop the bed. The walls were covered with beautiful paintings and tapestries, and each piece of art seemed perfect for its location. There were three windows with drapes covering them, and three doors. The room was so comfortable and inviting that it had a calming effect on me.

While l looked at the beauty of my surroundings, I became aware of voices off in the distance. I felt my panic buttons being activated again, but then soft, soothing music filled the air. I determined that the sounds were coming from outside the window to my left. I gathered up my courage and slowly approached the window. I then slowly pulled back the drapes just enough to see four people sitting at a table. I quickly stepped away from the window, more confused than ever. Where the hell was I? Who were those people? What was I doing here?

Being somewhat of a logical person, I commanded myself to think. The bright light—what could it mean? I remembered reading somewhere that when people die and are later revived, they report seeing a bright light. That must be it! I was dead. What else could it be? Wait a minute. I also remembered hearing that people who swore they were abducted by creatures from outer space also saw a bright light. Maybe that was it. Those people I saw were actually aliens! That must be it, I reasoned.

Convinced that I was either dead or abducted by aliens, I resigned myself to my fate. I was trying to decide which fate I preferred when I heard a soft tap on the door. I stood frozen, not knowing what to do. A child's voice said, "Are you okay, Joe?" I didn't respond, or I should say I couldn't respond. The voice continued, "My mom and dad would like you to join us in the garden."

There was something so disarming about the child's voice that I found myself being drawn to the door. I took a deep breath, told myself to remain calm, and then opened the door. There stood a boy about eight years old with the biggest grin I had ever seen. He seemed to be bursting with energy. His eyes were like two lightbulbs gleaming from a round, handsome face. He said, "Hello, my name is Michael," and reached out his hand. I took his hand without thinking. It was as if I was watching a movie. Michael led me to the others, who were outside in a large garden. I was surrounded by plants of all colors. There were fruit trees, flowers, and other plants with such pleasant aromas that I felt somewhat light-headed as I followed Michael.

We approached the people who were sitting around the table; they seemed relaxed and friendly. There were a number of children playing nearby. The adults and children stopped what they were doing as I neared, and they focused their attention on me. I must have had a comical look on my face, because they all started laughing as I stood there with my mouth open in a complete state of confusion. Their laughter was so good-natured that I found myself starting to laugh along with them.

Everything about my surroundings was so peaceful and friendly that I felt safe despite my confusion. After we all stopped laughing, the children continued with their game. A woman walked up to me, took my hand, and said, with a sweet, gentle voice, "You are truly welcome."

After a few seconds, I was finally able to blurt out, "I'm dead, aren't I?"

The four adults gave a knowing glance at each other and smiled. The woman who was still holding my hand said very reassuringly, "No, you are not dead."

I felt a sense of relief but was confused more than ever. "Then where am I?" I asked.

One of the men sitting at the table stood up and said, "I know this must be very confusing for you, but please be patient. We will explain everything in good time."

Their manner was so pleasant that I was somewhat hypnotized. I also noticed how healthy they all looked. Their skin almost glowed. They did not appear to have an ounce of fat on them. Their eyes twinkled, and their teeth gleamed as they all smiled at me.

The man then introduced himself, saying, "I am Peter."

The woman holding my hand introduced herself as Angela. The other man and woman introduced themselves as Richard and Rose. I started to introduce myself when Angela said, "We know who you are. We have been assigned to show you our community and answer any questions you may have."

Overwhelmed by curiosity and confusion, all I could say was, "Thank you."

Richard responded, "We will begin as soon as you have had a chance to freshen up," and then he called out to Michael, who was now playing with the other children. "Michael, would you please take Joe back to his room so he can clean up, then bring him to the study?"

Michael said, "Sure," grabbed my hand, and led me back to my room.

Once inside the room, Michael led me to a door and said, "The bathroom is in there." He then told me that I would find a change of clothes in a closet behind some sliding doors. He walked to the third door and said that he would be waiting outside.

After Michael left the room, I felt somewhat resigned and decided it would be best to go along with my hosts' wishes. I took a long, hot shower and dried myself with one of the softest towels I had ever used. Feeling refreshed, I opened the closet and found a shirt and a pair of pants that fit perfectly. Just as I finished dressing, Michael called out, "How are you doing, Joe?"

I opened the door to find the young boy eagerly awaiting me. He grabbed my hand and said, "Let's go." We walked down the long hallway as Michael told me that he liked to have visitors. He told me that when the adults were through showing me around, he would bring me to his secret spot, as long as I promised not to tell anyone where it was. I told him that I would be honored to see his secret hideaway and assured him that it would be our secret.

We entered a room filled with books, a desk, and several chairs. The four people I had met earlier were sitting by the desk and stood to greet me as I entered the room. Peter asked if I had found everything satisfactory. I told him that I was quite comfortable and ready to go. Angela asked if I was hungry. I hadn't thought about it but realized that I was starving. She said that they figured I would be.

I was led to the dining room, where several dishes of food were on a large table surrounded by chairs. We sat at the table, and I was handed a plate. There were several types of vegetables, fruits, nuts, cheeses, and breads to choose from. I filled my plate, sat back, and started to eat. As I looked around the room, I was once again struck by the beauty of the different artwork and furniture.

Rose seemed to be reading my mind and commented, "All the artwork you see are originals. The furniture is all handmade. Even the plate your food is on is handmade. We are a society of artists, craftspeople, farmers, musicians, and other professions that are based on individual expression. We mass-produce very few of the items necessary for our comfort." She continued, "We have discovered that the more we are able to reduce our use of machines, the better off we are. The goal of production is to produce items that will last. We have also discovered that when things are made by skilled craftspeople, with the proper resources, they last for several generations."

Angela chimed in, "For an example, the table we are sitting at is 120 years old. The longer it lasts, the more valuable it becomes."

After we finished eating, Peter suggested that we go on a tour of the community. I responded with an enthusiastic "Let's go!" that startled even me. Everybody smiled, looked at each other in a knowing way, and headed toward the door.

We exited the house onto a porch that overlooked a lawn. The lawn was surrounded by trees and shrubbery. I could hear sounds coming from beyond the foliage. It dawned on me how quiet it seemed. There was no sound of cars or trucks. All I could hear was the sound of birds singing, children playing, and the faint sound of music in the distance.

I followed my guides down a pathway to a gate. Walking through the gate, we entered a street. I could hardly believe my eyes. The street was approximately fifty yards wide. Across the street I could see the tops of houses that had different types of shrubbery, providing privacy for each home. The street itself was quite remarkable. There was a single track running down either side with a fence on both sides of each track. Alongside the tracks were two brick paths with people on bicycles going in both directions. Bordering the bicycle paths were benches with small shelters approximately every fifty feet.

We stopped at one of the shelters and sat on a bench. As people passed by, they would smile and greet us. Everyone seemed pleasant. No one spoke; we seemed to be waiting for something. We were there for only a few moments when I became aware of a sound coming from my left. Looking in the direction of the sound, I could see a trolley quietly rolling toward us. The trolley barely made a sound as it stopped in front of the shelter. I followed my guides onto the trolley. After we all sat down, as if by magic, the trolley quietly rolled away.

Peter explained to me that the trolley was the major form of transportation within the residential areas, which consisted of neighborhoods with approximately two hundred families. Each neighborhood had its own recreational facilities, schools, and medical center.

I asked how the trolley could move so quietly. Rose explained that the trolley was powered by an electrical current that ran through the rail. The electricity was generated from solar power, which supplied most of the energy needs of the entire community.

Looking around, I realized that no one was driving the trolley. I mentioned this fact, and Rose explained, "The trolley operates much like an elevator, in that it comes only when you call it. We activated the trolley when we sat on the bench at the calling station. When we sat down inside the trolley, we again activated the trolley. By pushing down on one of the armrests, we inform the trolley that we desire to stop."

I asked about cars, or, I should say, the lack thereof. I told them that I had never been in a place where I could neither hear nor see a car. They explained to me that they did have cars but they were not permitted within the residential areas. I learned that cars were stored outside the city limits and were only used for transportation to other cities or for pleasure trips.

The trolley came to a halt after traveling for about fifteen minutes. Peter told me that they would first show me their school, and with a great deal of pride, he pointed to a building about two hundreds yards away. Peter went on to explain, "Our children's education is our top priority. We believe that our major resource is our children. Therefore, we provide them with nurturing love and share with them the tools necessary to think for themselves so they can live happy, healthy lives."

He continued, "We view education as a never-ending process. We also believe that some form of discipline is necessary to grow and achieve. The more disciplined a person is, the more they grow and achieve. Only the individual can decide what effort they are willing to contribute to their own happiness.

"In a sense we view education as a training that develops self-control and character. We start that process in the child's home. The parents are responsible for teaching their children how to read and write. The parents are also responsible for their child's education until the age of about six. This age varies from child to child. Some children rapidly surpass their parents' abilities and need more advanced instruction. While the parents will always be a part of a child's education, the child would then be put into the school you are about to see."

Once Peter finished with his explanation, we started walking toward the school itself. I became aware of how pleasant everything seemed, as we entered a large playground area that consisted of a large field. The children were playing all sorts of games such as volleyball, baseball, and basketball. I marveled at how well manicured the grounds were.

I told Peter how impressed I was by the recreational facilities. He looked at me with a funny look in his eye and said, "We make recreation one of our three top priorities. We strongly encourage our children to play sports. Developing a child's body is of the utmost importance to us. We believe that sports are an excellent avenue for the child to learn about their bodies, the concept of teamwork, and the sense of personal accomplishment. We have found that sports provide many lessons in the search for happiness."

We entered the school through a narrow hallway, which opened to a large oval room. The sight was impressive. It was a room about fifty yards in diameter. About every twenty feet there were sections partitioned like pieces of a pie. Between each two partitions were different subject matters such as artwork; next to the art section was a music section with an assortment of musical instruments, then a space with maps and a globe, then a space that appeared to be for history, then a math section. There were also sections for the sciences and languages. The room had a large skylight, which brightened the room significantly. As a matter of fact, the room was so well lit that there were very few electric lights being used. There were also large windows in each section that provided light and plenty of cross ventilation.

Standing in the center of this amazing structure, I could see how the areas set aside for each subject provided privacy but yet encouraged free movement from area to area. A middle-aged man, who was working with a group of about six children, looked over at us and smiled. He joined our small party and greeted my guides, who in turn introduced me. Peter told him that I was a visitor and was on a tour of the community.

The teacher's manner was friendly, and he seemed eager to show me what he called the "Community Intermediate Learning Center." He began by telling me that the children who were at the center ranged from age five to thirteen. He stated that there were usually about a hundred students, with one teacher for every ten students. He went on to explain that parents were also required to spend one day a week at the center, assisting the "facilitators." When I looked puzzled over the word "facilitator," the teacher anticipated my question and went on to say, "We are not teachers in the sense that you are used to. We do not deposit information into the minds of our children and then require them to regurgitate that information back to us. We believe that nature has given each individual a special talent, and the purpose of education is to 'facilitate' or aid the individual in finding and developing that ability."

He went on to say, "Each child decides for themselves in what direction their talents will take them. As a facilitator, when a child begins to show an interest in a particular subject, we act as a resource in helping that child develop those interests."

He suggested that we follow him to one of the learning areas. After a few short steps, we seemed to be in a different world. There were several pieces of artwork at various stages of completion. A young boy caught my eye. He seemed oblivious to our presence and appeared to be putting the final touches on a painting. It was a beautiful depiction of children playing in the school yard, which was visible through the large window in the center of the room. I commented on how detailed and professional the painting looked.

The facilitator explained, "The boy is ten years old. He showed an interest in art when he was two years old. Both of his parents painted as a hobby, so it was only natural for them to encourage his interest. By the age of four, the boy had surpassed what his parents could show him. He started coming to the center three days a week after his fourth birthday. It was apparent from the beginning that his natural talent lies in his artwork. He has already outgrown the center and will require more advanced guidance. However, he will remain at the center until he completes his other studies."

I asked about a door that was located to the right of the window. I noticed a door in each section. The facilitator told me that there was a room off each learning section to provide more privacy. He said that currently there was a class going on in the private art room.

Peter interrupted, "Before we leave, why don't you explain what the curriculum is?"

The facilitator beamed as he said, "We believe that the purpose of the center is to help develop a whole child." He almost burst into laughter when he said, "That child painting over there would paint until his ears fell off!"

The child heard these comments and began to laugh. "We also require that he know something about the world he lives in, that he understands how his body works, what is good for it, and what is bad for it. We require that he has a working knowledge of mathematics, language, geography, history, and the sciences. In general we see this level of education as being a base from which the child develops some of the tools he or she will need to live a whole and happy life."

I asked the facilitator what would happen if a child did not show an interest in any of the areas offered. The facilitator and the others looked at me in disbelief. He said to me in a very serious manner, "That could never happen. The nature of humans is to seek knowledge. However, we never force a child to learn. We merely require that he or she is exposed to different subjects. If a child rejects the information being offered, we simply encourage him or her to keep an open mind. Ultimately, it is the child's choice."

I thought to myself that sure was different from the world I lived in. After giving the matter some thought, I discovered that I couldn't disagree. Rose said that there was still much to see and suggested that we move on. We said our good-byes, thanked the facilitator for his time, and headed for the exit.

Before I knew it, we were back on the trolley, silently gliding toward a new destination. My mind was still back at the learning center, thinking to myself how different things were in this strange place, when the trolley came to a stop. I looked around and realized that we were in what appeared to be a large marketplace.

After exiting the trolley, I found myself standing in the middle of a small park that was surrounded by several shops and restaurants. There were several hundred people walking around. The atmosphere was exciting yet relaxed. I had never experienced anything like what I was seeing. The place had the excitement of a big city without the usual noise. Everybody seemed to be having a good time. Rose explained, "This is the major trading center for the city. Everything a person could possibly need could be found in one of the 432 shops in the surrounding area."

We entered a very charming little café. The café was bigger than it appeared from the outside. There were three musicians playing soft jazz. They were very good. My guides took me to a table near the band, and we all sat down. The music was intoxicating. The café was decorated with an assortment of murals and stained-glass windows. There were also bookshelves along the walls. The tables and chairs were all made of wood and had that handmade look. It must have been the lunch hour, because the place was filled with customers.

Peter came to the table with a large tray filled with drinks, some cut-up vegetables, and an assortment of cheeses, bread, and some dried fish. I eagerly grabbed my drink and took a big gulp. It was delicious. I never tasted anything like it. It was some type of fruit drink, but I could not tell what it was made of. I was told that the drink was the specialty of the house. It was made from fresh fruit grown locally, squeezed and made on the premises. The owner refused to share the recipe, so this was the only place in the city that you could get such a treat.

I sat there sipping my fruit drink, nibbling at the food, and listening to the music. I felt relaxed. The band took a break as we sat in a peaceful state; Peter looked at me and said, "As was previously mentioned, our economy is based on the small shop owners, craftspeople, farmers, and artists. We limit the material goods that require mass production. The factories are located at a safe distance from the residential areas and are in operation three months out of the year. Those who contribute their labor in these factories work only those three months. This is because factory work is so repetitive and monotonous that three months is enough for anybody."

Peter went on to explain that almost everything was produced by hand. Virtually all the furniture, clothes, jewelry, rugs, and any other of the goods essential to a quality life were handmade in the small workshops located within walking distance from the shopowner's home. The more items that a person desired, the more he or she had to contribute to the community at large.

Rose joined in and said, "Each city is self-contained. Cities were planned around the surrounding environment. Cities were built taking into account things such as access to drinking water, farmland, and natural resources such as trees. The goal of each community is self-reliance. We believe that the less material goods we need, the freer we become. Our communities embody that philosophy."

I asked what they did when they could not produce something that they needed. Angela told me, "We work in cooperation with the other communities. Our society is structured in such a way that first comes the community. The goal of each community is self-reliance. However, because each community is unique, it has something different to offer. For example, let us say that one community is rich in timber and another community is an ideal place to grow corn. The two communities exchange their products to the mutual benefit of both. These exchanges take place on several levels. Not only are products exchanged between communities, there are cultural exchanges as well. Things such as music, dance, plays, artwork, and books are shared between the different communities."

Angela passionately continued, "Since we believe that all living things are connected and dependent on each other for their survival, we naturally believe that all communities are dependent on each other. We also believe that all communities have something in common. That is the pursuit of happiness.

"Each community has a government that consists of a representative from each neighborhood. Each neighborhood meets once a week to discuss mutual concerns. At this level most disputes are handled, such as when behavior occurs that might disrupt the peace or when an individual is not contributing their fair share but is still reaping the benefits of the community. From each neighborhood, a representative is selected to meet with other neighborhood representatives and discuss mutual concerns. Each community varies in size, but we have found that communities of about twenty thousand people is optimum. This number provides enough diversity to produce the goods necessary without becoming cumbersome."

Rose took it from there, saying, "The community governments meet once a month unless an emergency arises. The next level of government is the state government. The state government consists of representatives of about twenty communities. Other factors such as geography play a part in determining the makeup of the state government, but rarely does the state rise above five hundred thousand people. This government also meets once a month, unless a special session is called.

"The next level of government is the central government, which consists of a representative for each state government. The central government's role is a relatively minor one, in that most problems are first handled on the neighborhood level. Those problems that cannot be handled on the neighborhood level are usually settled at the community level, then state level. The governments are based on the belief that the whole cannot be healthy unless each of its individual components is healthy."

Peter joined in. "The last in the chain of governments is the world government. The world government is based on the belief that all people of the world want to be happy!" At this point I realized several people in the restaurant had been listening in on our conversation and were nodding in agreement.

There was a festive mood, with several people breaking out in conversation. I had never had a feeling of such camaraderie and friendliness. After a few minutes of hand-shaking and good cheer, Angela suggested that we move on.

Once outside the restaurant, I was again moved by how beautiful the town was. There were trees lining the streets with trolleys silently gliding past shops. We began walking down the main road. The first shop we came to was a shoe store. There was an assortment of shoes in the window. I was drawn to the window like a metal to a magnet. I was taken aback by the beauty of the shoes. As I stood there looking through the window, someone suggested that we go inside to try a few pairs on.

I became self-conscious and protested that I had no money. Besides, the shoes looked far too expensive. All the guides smiled and assured me that it would be okay. Entering the shop, I observed shelves all along the sides with two rows of shelves running down the middle. All the shelves were filled with shoes. I expected to see a salesperson but no one seemed to be in the shop.

I turned to Rose and expressed my concern, saying, "Anybody could walk in and help themselves." The guides all said in unison, "Exactly."

Then Rose said, in a voice that sounded like a soft flute, "The shoes that you see before you and all the goods in all the shops in town were handmade by local craftspeople. As long as people contribute to the good of the whole, they can take what they need."

She continued in her sing-song manner, "The craftspeople usually have a shop in their home, but when power tools are required, each trade has whatever tools necessary in each shop. Depending on the craft, there could be as many as five craftspeople in each shop. Each individual's desire to produce determines how much they could take in return. As you can see, this is a very productive shop. The owners of this shop have earned enough credits to travel. They are currently touring different parts of the world with their families."

I could not help but ask, "You mean there is no one to monitor who takes what or how much a person takes?"

Peter responded, "Not in the sense you are asking. People who contribute less do so because they desire less. Even when a person contributes more, this does not mean they do so because of their desire for more material goods. If a person begins to take more than they deserve, they could be brought before the neighborhood council to have the matter resolved."

I found myself thinking about what a strange place I was in: shops without salespeople, where you take what you want. How odd. This was certainly like no place on earth that I was familiar with. Then all of a sudden, my eyes caught a beautiful pair of shoes that seemed to appear from nowhere. I found myself reaching for these shoes. I caught myself and realized what I was doing. Rose complimented me on my choice. I tried to protest, saying that I never contributed anything to their community, but they insisted.

I reluctantly reached for the shoes, but once I touched them, I quickly got over my apprehension. They were a soft grayish brown, made of a sturdy fabric, and woven in an intricate pattern that made them seem more like works of art than something I would put on my feet. I sat in a nearby chair and slipped off the sandals I was wearing. I held the shoes in my hands for a few seconds and then put them on.

It was like putting on a pair of socks. I smiled with pleasure, telling my guides that I had never put a pair of shoes on that felt so comfortable. I asked what type of material that the shoes were made out of. Peter explained, "The primary source of most of our fabrics is hemp. Hemp is the primary source of many of the goods you will see in the shops. Of course, there are other materials such as cotton and silk for clothes, but hemp was the most durable and easiest to grow. The soles are made from rubber. We rely on renewable sources for approximately 89 percent of all goods produced."

I reluctantly started to take the shoes off when Angela said quietly, "Please, keep those shoes as a memento of your visit. After all, they were made especially for you."

I started to ask how this could be, when our attention was drawn outside the shoe store by music and laughter. The guides looked at each other and smiled. Peter gleefully said, "It's festival time!"

We quickly left the shop and walked into an amazing scene. There were hundreds of people in the streets, dancing and singing. Looking past the crowd of people, I could see several trolley cars filled to the brim with fresh fruits and vegetables. The guides took turns explaining to me what was going on. "The trolleys arrive every day from the local farms. The farms work on a rotational basis, supplying an ample amount of produce for the needs of the entire community. While we do import some food, we do so out of the desire to eat various things that cannot be grown or produced locally. Our climate and soil produce some of the sweetest fruits in the world. We exchange these fruits and the products we create from our fruit for other products from around the world."

As we were talking, the trolleys were being quickly emptied. The produce was brought to nearby grocery stores. Rose asked me if I was interested in seeing the farmland. "Why not?" was all I could say. At this point I felt as if I were floating through time. We climbed up on a trolley and once again were going on a new adventure.

After a short ride, we were out of the shopping area. We entered yet another park. This park was bigger than the first park. It had more activities going on. There were several baseball games and soccer games, all happening at the same time. I could see tennis courts, basketball courts, and a huge swimming pool full of splashing people. A guide had mentioned earlier that these people take their recreation very seriously; they were not exaggerating.

I sat back and reflected about all that I was experiencing. I had never felt so peaceful. There was beauty all around me. From the moment I woke up, I had been surrounded by beautiful things and beautiful people. I had not heard a hostile word or sound. All I heard were the sounds of nature or people laughing and singing.

As my mind was basking in a sense of calm, I became aware of a sweet, wonderful aroma. I realized that the landscape had changed dramatically. We were now gliding through a forest of large trees. The odors were incredible!

A few moments later, we entered a large grove of peach trees. Rose looked at me and said proudly, "These are the best peaches in the world."

I had no reason to doubt her. As we reached the top of a rise, I could see that peach trees extended as far as the eye could see. I could also see a large house not far from where our trolley had stopped. There was a field of tomatoes fronting the house. I could see people sitting on a large porch. The people saw us and waved. The guides responded in kind. I found myself also waving. I felt as if I belonged in this place.

Once again Rose said, with a great deal of pride, "Our food supply is the most important aspect to the health of our community! We grow enough food within the distance you have traveled today to feed our community a nutritious, well-balanced diet. As you know, we also grow plants that provide raw material for our clothes, our housing materials, and even our fuels. The peaches you see are a crop that we use for export. We produce jams, we dry it, and we make wine and liquors. Other communities produce things for export. We trade with each other to provide us with the diversity necessary to make life pleasurable.

"Each farmer is given an area that they are responsible for, to produce food for the entire community. The farmers work in cooperation with each other. The farmers determine such things as irrigation, what type of fertilizers to use, what crops to plant, and so on. Machinery is shared. The goal of every farmer is to produce as much food as possible within the laws of nature."

I sat in the trolley with my guides, taking in this panoramic beauty. I thought to myself, what a wonderful place I found myself in, a place where everybody had plenty of good food to eat and spent a good part of their day playing, socializing, or just relaxing—a place where everybody had a good education and meaningful work. It seemed as though these people had eliminated most of the bad things that happened where I came from.

I knew that there was no place on earth that I was aware of that had achieved the type of harmony these people seemed to enjoy. Then it hit me like a ton of bricks. The bright light! I was no longer on earth! I had been abducted by aliens! My guides must have seen the panicked look on my face, because they all asked me what was wrong. In a breathless voice, I was finally able to say, "I am no longer on earth, am I?"

The guides all came up to me and hugged me. A sense of relief came over me. I knew in that moment that no matter what the explanation was, I could be happy in this place. Finally Rose said, "We know that you are confused. It's time we took you back to our home and explained everything."

The trolley took off as if it was reading our thoughts. I decided to absorb as much of what I was seeing as possible, trying not to think about what I was going to be told. We passed through the peach fields, then the forest, into the park, past the shops, the school, then slowly, soundlessly came to a stop where we began our journey.

Michael was playing with some children in the front yard when he saw us getting off the trolley. He came running up and said, "It's about time you guys got home!"

We all smiled at him, saying that we had a very pleasant trip. The guides asked Michael if he would mind keeping me company for a few minutes while they took care of some business. Rose looked at me and said, "We will be right back and explain everything."

I watched as my four guides walked away, wondering why they didn't just tell me what's going on, when Michael, bursting with enthusiasm, said, "Perfect. While they're gone, I can show you my secret place!"

I was anxious to find out what was going on and didn't want to go anywhere until the guides came back, but Michael looked at me so pleadingly I could not say no. I told him that I would go with him but that I didn't want to be gone long. He assured me that we would only be gone a short while, grabbed my arm, and away we went.

We quickly walked down a small path that narrowed as we went through some bushes. We came upon several large trees. Nestled in these trees was a well-hidden tree house. Michael told me that this was his secret hideaway that only his best friends were allowed to visit. He explained that usually no adults were allowed but he wanted me to see it.

He bounded up the ladder leading to the tree house and beckoned me to join him. I'm not really fond of heights but felt that I couldn't disappoint my little friend. I reluctantly started to climb toward the tree house, making sure that I didn't look down. Reaching the tree house was a great relief. Once inside, I was immediately taken by the view. The sun was setting behind the community we had just visited. Just then, we heard Peter calling us.

Michael panicked and whispered, "We can't let them find us. I'll cut them off!" Before I could say anything, he was already halfway down the ladder. He looked at me and yelled, "Hurry!"

I told him that I would be right behind him. I started down the ladder and, without thinking, made a critical mistake. I looked down. I became terrified, lost my grip, and began to fall. I closed my eyes as I fell, waiting for the thud, when all of a sudden I felt a bang on my nose.

As I slowly opened my eyes, I saw a small boy standing over me with a beach ball in his hands. He said, "Sorry, mister."

CHAPTER NINE

All You Have to Do Is Dream

IN CONCLUSION, I FEEL it is necessary to say that I wrote this book without any expectation other than speaking my mind. I truly believe that the world we live in can be anything we want to be as long as we work together.

I have not used footnotes in composing this book, but I have borrowed many ideas from several authors. Jeremy Rifkin's *Entropy* helped me understand one of the basic laws of nature: that you can neither create nor destroy energy. All we can do is change things from a usable state to a nonusable state. Mortimer J. Adler's book *We Hold These Truths* was the basis for my definition of happiness being a whole life lived well. This book was invaluable to me in providing a basis for many of my ideas in this book. Kirkpatrick Sale's book *The Human Scale* convinced me that whenever anything—whether it be a person, place, or thing—becomes too big, it becomes a negative instead of a positive. Paulo Freire's book *Pedagogy of the Oppressed* inspired me with his definition of the true meaning of education. Henry Bamford Parkes's book

The American Experience, was very insightful in showing that there was not this monolithic American consciousness but several worldviews that created who we are as a people. *American Sphinx* by Joseph J. Ellis was very helpful in my understanding the mind of the author of the Declaration of Independence, Thomas Jefferson. I also relied on my *New American Desk Encyclopedia* for some fact-checking.

In a sense I borrowed bits and pieces from all of these books. However, I feel it is important for me to state that this book is based on the belief that all people—young, old, black, white, Asian, rich, poor, educated, noneducated, women, and men—all have the same needs. Until we meet the basic needs of all human beings, none of us will be safe, healthy, or happy.